Writing Through Bereavement

This workbook is designed to help bereaved parents find words for grief in their quest for well-being after the devastating death of a child by offering a hands-on approach to therapeutic writing that can be used as a means of self-help, in collaboration with therapists, or in the context of support groups featuring writing for well-being.

The book presents a seven-week therapeutic writing program that integrates field-tested writing techniques with general psychoeducation around grief and related emotions as well as the quest for meaning in a life transformed by loss. Each module shares a common structure, checking in with the writer, introducing a theme for the week, and providing specific prompts to safely engage the loss, explore the emotions it engenders, and foster more adaptive meaning-making about a devastating life experience. Readers are given the opportunity to tailor the brief immersive writing to their unique circumstances and to respond to reflective questions that invite greater clarity and self-compassion as they attempt to re-enter life following loss. In this respect, the book acknowledges the diversity of ways that parents can adapt to the loss of a child and offers practical counsel and self-reflective tools to support them in this effort.

Bereaved parents, grandparents, and family members will find the workbook to be a valuable resource as they work to cope with their grief. It will also be of use to professionals who want to facilitate writing courses for bereaved parents or provide them with individual support.

Olga V. Lehmann, PhD, is a psychotherapist, educator, and mental health activist, as well as an associate professor in psychology at the University of Stavanger (Norway).

Robert A. Neimeyer, PhD, is a professor emeritus at the University of Memphis, and director of the Portland Institute for Loss and Transition. Neimeyer has published 35 books, including *New Techniques of Grief Therapy: Bereavement and Beyond*, and edits the Routledge Series on *Death, Dying and Bereavement*.

Trine Giving Kalstad, MSc, is a social anthropologist and cognitive therapist who has, since 2001, been the director of public health and bereavement support in The Norwegian SIDS and Stillbirth Society (LUB). She is currently a PhD fellow at the Centre of Crisis Psychology, University of Bergen.

'This book is a heart centered invitation to do the important soul work of grieving. What I appreciated so much was how this book approached grief with mindful compassion and tenderness. It will be salve to many grieving parents.'

Dr. Joanne Cacciatore, *Professor, Arizona State University, Director of the Graduate Certificate in Trauma and Bereavement Program andnFounder, MISS Foundation and Selah Carefarm*

'Although much has been written about grieving and how we might survive the loss of a child, few resources have been available about how to deal with such a devastating bereavement. This therapeutic writing workbook respects the magnitude of child loss and takes parents through a process where they may make meaning as they honour their experience and create new ground for wellbeing. This is a valuable and heartfelt resource founded in evidence-based research on child death.'

Dr. Reinekke Lengelle, *Associate Professor, Athabasca University, curriculum designer of writing for wellbeing, author of* Writing the Self in Bereavement: A Story of Love, Spousal Loss and Resilience, *and co-editor of* Writing for Wellbeing: Theory, Research and Practice

'A deeply humane companion to grief, which demonstrates the powerful potential of creativity in bereavement. *Writing Through Bereavement* offers detailed, compassionate and holistic guidance built upon years of experience, and it makes exemplary use of theory, presenting complex ideas lightly, accessibly and never without practical relevance to readers' own experiences. A much-needed book which I will strongly recommend to the grieving families I work with, and those who support them.'

Dr Tamarin Norwood, *Doctoral Prize Research Fellow, Loughborough University UK, Author of the memoir* The Song of the Whole Wide World *about parenthood and bereavement*

Writing Through Bereavement

A Therapeutic Workbook for Grieving Parents

Olga V. Lehmann, Robert A. Neimeyer
and Trine Giving Kalstad

Routledge
Taylor & Francis Group

LONDON AND NEW YORK

Designed cover image: Lars Ravn Ohlckers, Untitled, acrylic on paper, 2023
Reproduced with permission from the artist.

First published 2025
by Routledge
4 Park Square, Milton Park, Abingdon, Oxon OX14 4RN

and by Routledge
605 Third Avenue, New York, NY 10158

Routledge is an imprint of the Taylor & Francis Group, an informa business

© 2025 Olga V. Lehmann, Robert A. Neimeyer and Trine Giving Kalstad

British Library Cataloguing-in-Publication Data
A catalogue record for this book is available from the British Library

ISBN: 978-1-032-72971-8 (hbk)
ISBN: 978-1-032-71459-2 (pbk)
ISBN: 978-1-003-42327-0 (ebk)

DOI: 10.4324/9781003423270

Typeset in Optima
by KnowledgeWorks Global Ltd.

Contents

Foreword

The book you hold in your hands is only half-written. The words the authors have written usefully summarize professional knowledge about grief. They offer lists of words that you might use to tell your story. The most interesting words on their lists might be those you react to as not describing how you feel if you think about why. What counts throughout the book is that the authors' words enable you to write the half of this book that is now empty.

Grief is often described as an emptiness. Writing that, I wonder how many readers would not describe their grief that way. If a reader thinks, "No, not emptiness, more like …," that may be more valuable than accepting the word emptiness as a description of grief. But although I have never known a grief anything like the death of one of my children, the description of emptiness fits the griefs I have known.

This emptiness presents a paradox: it can never be filled, yet as life goes on, it does fill or becomes less empty. Some people's grief may be so extreme that they find the idea of filling the emptiness to be intolerable. Those people need, I think, a companionship that exceeds what any book can offer, and I hope they find that help. But for those readers who accept that emptiness will fill, even though some part always remains empty, the question is what will fill that emptiness.

This book offers guidance in how to fill the emptiness not as you choose – the idea of choice seems out of place in grief – but as you intend, if an intention is a direction toward, though never fully realized. The writing exercises that I imagine will be most useful are those that reconnect parents to their children, such as writing a letter to a deceased child. Emptiness then fills – if never being filled – with continuing caring.

What I believe grieving people want most is to find ways to continue to express caring for their loved one who has died. Some parents practice rituals at their child's grave; some engage in charitable work to help other children. Some support other grieving parents. This book helps parents to continue to express caring through writing.

Thus the value of this book is in the blank spaces when the authors' words end and the reader becomes the writer. The recommended writing is, at first, broken down into small bits, single sentences, maybe just words not yet formed into sentences. How far anyone's writing progresses, even beyond the exercises in this book, depends on you, each individual reader. As you do various writing exercises – or decide not to do certain exercises – the book can help you learn what you need, or don't need, or might need later but not now.

I wish for each of this book's readers that you can find someone else, preferably someone with whom you share the continuing love of your child, and do this writing with them: writing together, maybe reading each other what you have written. At times you may just sit together in silence because in that silence, some part of your mind will be discovering how you need to tell your story. Over time, although that silence will always be sad, may the continuing love between you and your child make it a space of sufficient comfort.

Arthur W. Frank, Ph.D., FRSC
Professor Emeritus, University of Calgary, Canada

Acknowledgments

We want to express our heartfelt appreciation to each of the parents who enrolled in the five courses in which we piloted and refined this workbook, as they shared their stories, their reflections about the process of writing, and their feedback on what worked well and what could be improved in subsequent courses. We are especially grateful to Nina Vennevold, Liv Marie Baden, Colin MacKenzie, Bjørn Anders Reutz, and Ingunn Moen for their support and detailed feedback on earlier drafts of the workbook. It is a better and more useful tool for bereaved parents as a result.

We also thank Reinekke Lengelle for the support she provided us as a co-supervisor for the initial pilots of our courses, in which she generously shared her wisdom and recommendations as a leading contributor to the burgeoning field of writing for wellbeing. Last but not least, we want to express our appreciation to the DAM Foundation and the LUB Research Fund in Norway for providing us with the economic support to carry on with the research and development of the online courses, and this very workbook as one of its fruits.

We also thanks Sandra Blikås/ByHand and LUB for the permission to use the illustrations on pages 8, 30, 46, 58, 71, 85, 98.

Thanks to Lars Ravn Ohlckers for allowing us to use a picture of his work of art for us to use it as a cover.

Most of the royalties of this book will be donated to the research fund of the Norwegian SIDS and Stillbirth Society.

Therapeutic writing through bereavement

An introduction

Therapeutic writing is one of many tools available to help us when we experience tragic events, such as the death of a child. As we experience such tragedy, we can feel deeply vulnerable: alone, ashamed, misunderstood, or helpless. To write can then become a form of dialogue with ourselves, for ourselves, and about ourselves, which can help us cope with difficult events, feelings, thoughts, and behaviors. Writing can support us as we seek meaning and motivation despite having our world shattered unexpectedly.

When a child dies, embracing self-compassion, hope, and acceptance is often easier said than done. We have written this workbook together with, and for, bereaved parents. We wanted to craft practices to accompany parents in the arduous process of living a life without the physical presence of their children. What started as a small pilot program during the COVID-19 pandemic in 2020 has become a larger project with the needs and wants of each of our participants in focus.

We have had two main objectives with the writing courses we have arranged as we developed this workbook. The first was to increase the writers' *window of tolerance* for the painful emotions that are part and parcel of the loss of a child, permitting them to be in contact with grief long enough to learn to navigate it, and to grow in compassion for self and others through the experience. The second goal was to affirm the writers' ongoing relationship and attachment to their children, despite their physical death. Of course, we realize that drawing close to the pain and their child is a brave act, and can naturally trigger resistance and tension. We therefore are already grateful for your courage in opening this book, being here, and being willing to write from a heart that has been broken by unspeakable loss.

Based on our experience as therapists, as well as our insights in developing and evaluating the writing courses that were a foundation for this workbook, we have witnessed the many challenges that bereaved parents face in finding adequate support for their grief. Even if there are major differences between healthcare systems in different contexts, studies suggest that about two-thirds of bereaved parents do not receive the support they feel they need (Aoun et al., 2015). Some of this support regards the process of finding meaning in life despite the loss, as well as the opportunity to process turbulent emotions that are difficult to put into words.

We have structured this workbook as a seven-week program that combines writing sessions for approximately 2–3 hours each, as well as follow-up exercises you can explore between sessions. The contents of this workbook are the fruit of 4 years of collaboration between the authors, Olga Lehmann, Robert A. Neimeyer, and Trine G. Kalstad, as well as with Reinekke Lengelle in the early pilot projects. We actively included the experiences and feedback from over 60 participants of five online therapeutic writing courses, negotiating the length, intensity, and contents of the course directly with the parents who

DOI: 10.4324/9781003423270-1

participated. Some of the techniques have been widely used in grief therapy, whereas others we have either created or adapted to address important emotions and goals relevant to parental bereavement. We hope that the program will offer you experiences of insight, healing, love, and resilience, as it has for many others. We honor the need for continuous research and development in this field and we are therefore curious for further studies that can address the further implementation potential of this workbook as well as possibilities to improve it in future editions.

Each of the weeks has an objective, concrete practices, and brief sections with psychoeducation about grief as an inseparable aspect of life. This weekly orientation serves as a compass for navigating a sea of suffering and uncertainty, in a quest for new and solid ground on which to rebuild a life in the wake of a precious life that has been lost. In the first week, you will be introduced to grief and therapeutic writing, as well as the essential role of hope. The second week explores resistance toward writing and what grieving can teach us about life. In the third week, we focus on dialogue, as well as the ways in which our identity shapes the dialogues we have with different parts of ourselves, and as well as with others. The fourth week brings emotions such as anger, guilt, and shame into focus through the lenses of compassion and self-compassion. The fifth week has to do with reciprocity and our relationship with love and grief. We will address both how grief affects the way we live, and how life affects the way we grieve. In the sixth week, we will focus on the relationship between personal values and meaning in life. Last but not least, in the seventh week we will continue to work on finding meaning in life, and how to continue the bond with your child.

How to use this book

If you are using this book as part of a facilitator-led therapeutic writing group, whether onsite or online, we strongly recommend that you follow the course of the program week by week, chapter by chapter, because the practices build upon each other. In addition to the weekly sessions, we have suggested some homework assignments that you can optionally explore in between sessions. If for any reason you choose not to write between sessions, keep a friendly and curious attitude and ask yourself what is holding you back from writing. Throughout the book, you'll encounter shaded boxes that suggest **guidelines to group practice,** which can help create the sense of safety, respect, and honesty that all participants will need to do and share their writing, as well as suggestions for how to keep time and facilitate sharing. We've organized **each chapter to correspond with a 2 to 3-hour weekly group meeting,** with two short breaks for a snack or self-care. Many of our participants in our study groups have remarked that the group sharing made a strong contribution to their learning about grief and adaptation after the death of a child (Lehmann et al., 2022; Lehmann, Kalstad & Neimeyer, 2023), and we hope you will participate actively if you are engaged in this sort of group experience. We are aware that not all bereaved parents will be able to join a group but still, we have the hope that this book will be a foundation for the development of more therapeutic writing groups worldwide, as well as more research about it in the field of grief.

If you are using this book on your own, we encourage you to use this workbook as a bridge to deepen your connection with others, so that the observations or insights that arise for you in using the book also find their way into meaningful conversations with your spouse, family, a therapist, a fellow bereaved parent, or other supportive persons. Of course, if you are using this book in a self-guided way, you can choose the pacing of the writing that works for you. For example, even if you use our suggestions about how long to write in relation to the various prompts, questions, and exercises, you could choose to "chunk" the chapters into smaller segments, rather than doing all the writing in a single 2-3-hour sitting as in the group context. Even though you will have discretion about when to write, when to pause, and when to shift attention to other things, we would encourage you to consider the following guidelines:

- *Write for at least 15–30 minutes at a time.* Research suggests doing so promotes greater insight and mastery of traumatic experiences *(Pennebaker & Smyth, 2016).,* whereas very brief writing about difficult topics followed by "escape" to another activity promotes only greater anxiety or avoidance.
- *Follow the order of the exercises within chapters, and of chapters within the workbook.* Each writing directive is designed to build on those that came before and to better prepare you for those that will follow. Skipping randomly through the various questions and exercises is likely to limit the usefulness of the workbook for you.
- *Create a "safe" space for the work.* This should include finding a time and place that feels comfortable where you will not be interrupted, and if you are working on your laptop or a tablet, be sure to turn off notifications, email, and other distractions. We give other suggestions of a practical kind for setting the stage and tone for the writing below.
- *Plan transitions into writing and back into life.* Therapeutic writing can take you to a deep, sometimes emotional, and even sacred space that is very different from everyday life. If you choose to write in short sessions, we recommend you to do the warm-up practices and the check-out every time you sit and write. This will help you have a transition in and out of the writing session, as well as some insight into what is happening at that very moment. In addition, as you complete a writing session, whether it is 20 minutes, 3 hours, or something in between, have in mind a way of setting down the pen and gradually shifting your attention from your inner to your outer world. Some people meditate for a few minutes, perform yoga or gentle stretching, take a walk or run, listen to music that gradually activates them, or join a friend for coffee, tea, or conversation. You might experiment with different transitions to see what works best for you.
- *Respect your window of tolerance.* Even if you have the best of intentions when sitting and writing, opening grief's door is a daunting experience. In addition, writing can make us feel anxious because when we pen words about the loss onto paper, it can feel more real. Be kind with yourself, especially if tears arise, or intense memories take over. Pause when necessary. Mind the rhythm of your breath and slow it down.
- *Have a low-threshold for seeking support.* If you feel too overwhelmed or transiting dark and unbearable hours, call someone close or a grief hotline if you need a listening ear. Even if you feel alone in the dark abyss of your grief, you are not alone. Support is available somewhere. At the end of this workbook, we have included a list with several organizations worldwide, those we are aware exists although there might be many more.

We also encourage you to find your own voice and rhythm during the writing itself. As obvious as this statement might sound, you will find yourself wordless at times, and other times, writing what you think others want to hear. It is important that you navigate each writing effort at your own pace. Some days you will find yourself writing non-stop and some other days you will stare at a blank page and feel numb, or afraid. Sitting and daring to find words for grief can be as daunting as it is validating or liberating. If you feel overwhelmed by difficult emotions, take a pause, do a grounding practice, or call someone you can talk about what you are feeling. When we are suffering, we can forget to take care of ourselves. Be as kind to yourself as humanly possible and find a balance between challenging yourself to tolerate the darkness you are going through, and finding a way to connect with other aspects of life. If resistance keeps being your main feeling session by session, ask yourself, *what are my core motivations to engage in a program of therapeutic writing? What are my expectations? What made me think of writing as a tool to work through your grief?* Writing in response to those questions might get the ink flowing, in a sense, about other aspects of your grief experience. You might also find it useful to talk with others about it.

Some of the practices that we use in this book received permission from their authors for non-profit use to help the bereaved. We hope you will respect the copyright on these materials, and we encourage you to contact the authors if you have any questions about the appropriate use of these exercises. Of course, we hope you will find the book useful personally and, if you are a therapist or bereavement support facilitator, that you appropriately credit the authors when presenting or citing this workbook in professional contexts.

Please reach out to us with your experiences, and let us know if you want to receive facilitation training with us, or collaborate on our ongoing research on these writing procedures.

Practical information

Before sitting down to write, gather your materials together so you have what you need in one place. This helps ensure that you can engage with the writing exercises as undisturbed as humanly possible. In addition to this workbook, you might want to have:

- Sufficient paper and pens/pencils. We suggest you have a notebook devoted to these practices in which you can write or make notes, as many parents find that a chronological record of their writing becomes a rich resource as they move forward, and an evolving record of their progress. Some parents prefer to write on digital devices. If this applies to you, we suggest you have a folder on your computer where you can store your drafts, which will of course be automatically dated for your later referencing.
- Something to drink such as water, coffee, or tea.
- A snack, such as chocolate, fruits, or nuts.
- A blanket and a pillow, as you want to feel comfortable if you sit for longer periods of time.
- Some parents light a candle as a symbol of connecting with their children and themselves. Blowing it out at the end of the writing also can help mark the conclusion of the writing period, just as it would do any other meaningful ritual.
- Some parents have a picture of their children, especially when the writing focuses on the relationship. At other times, they might prefer to have such an image out of sight, giving themselves "permission" to focus purely on their own emotions, on other relationships, on the future, or on other topics. You might just experiment with this, and see what feels right to you.

Guidelines for Group Practice

If you are using this workbook as part of a writing group, whether online or onsite, you will likely benefit from implementing or observing some important guidelines for the group process. The following group rules are based on our professional experience, as well as inspired by helpful principles for group facilitation such as those suggested in Palmer and Scribner's (2017), and mindfulness-based programs (e.g., Chozen Bays, 2017). Remember that group dynamics take time to be established and you might want to review these group guidelines more than once during the first sessions of the course.

Of course, each facilitator might want to adapt these guidelines to fit the goals and context of the group in question.

- **Respect confidentiality.** Group members should refrain from sharing with others outside of the group context whatever is said by their participants, except their own individual contributions. Do not assume that participants know this basic principle because you do. Many parents might be ambivalent about opening up and sharing their most vulnerable memories, thoughts, beliefs, or emotions, and the assurance of privacy will help create the safety they need to risk disclosure and sharing.
- **Solicit consent.** If you are conducting a course on therapeutic writing that is part of a research project, make sure to have participants read and sign a consent form that explains the purpose of the project, as well as how their personal data will be treated.
- **Encourage a first-person focus.** Ask members to speak only of their own personal experiences, using, for example, I-statements such as "I feel…," "When I wrote this, I…," "During this practice, I noticed that…"
- **Discourage advice.** Some members might notice the impulse to give advice or tell others what they should do or not do when grieving. When this happens, just encourage the member to notice that urge and even write about it. In general, note that these groups emphasize "holding space and respecting others experience" rather than teaching, directing, or advising other mourners.
- **Foster turn-taking.** Ensure that members take turns to listen with an open heart. By this we mean to have the intention to listen to understand, to hold space for others.
- **Offer feedback.** As a facilitator, you can share non-evaluative comments about the texts written during the sessions, and specific suggestions on how to do so are provided throughout the book. Likewise, it is fine for members to share how it is for them to listen to someone else's story. However, when a person is sharing, comments should be limited to appreciative reactions or honest questions without "right" answers, rather than digressions into the stories of the commentator.
- **Emphasize support over analysis.** Remember that this is not group therapy. As a facilitator, you might or might not have a clinical background, but in either case, your main role is to support members in their writing practices. If you have a sense that a given person might need specialized support, approach them discreetly with this suggestion outside the group context. Similarly, you might make this recommendation during the screening when discussing the various forms of support the interviewee might need.
- **Respect ownership of the writing.** Each group member holds the rights to her or his own writings. You can encourage participants but never require them to share some of what they have written with one another because the process of sharing

can help them feel and be understood and to integrate grief into their everyday lives. Sharing can help parents find meaning in the loss experience and can create a sense of togetherness between participants. It also provides an opportunity to raise awareness – including your own – about what the writers need, or the places where they are stuck. But to write freely and without self-censorship, members should be assured that they have the right to choose what to share of their writing, and what to hold private.

- **Consider the pros and cons of social media**. Encourage members to evaluate whether or not their texts are ready to be shared on social media platforms, or with family members and friends. This is a personal choice and only the authors themselves can determine their readiness to "go public" about their private writing for well-being. Once the writings are out and published it is difficult to take them back. Discuss with the group the likelihood that some people might understand exactly what the posting author meant, but others could also misinterpret and judge them.
- **Reinforce attendance.** It is important to emphasize the importance of attending all sessions, as they build upon each other, and consistency in showing up reinforces group cohesion and trust. In case something happens that delays a member or precludes their attendance, ask that they inform you as soon as possible.

When participating in an online group

- **Arrive early.** Check the internet connection beforehand. Connect 10 minutes before the session starts, especially during the first encounter. It is important to have all the online setups in place and make sure your audio and camera work fine. This will ensure that the sessions start in a timely fashion and that technicalities can be sorted in due time.
- **Eliminate distractions.** Make sure to close other windows and programs on your computer or telephone in order to avoid distractions. Reinforce the same practice among group members to make the space for each session to be as quiet and calm as possible.
- **Choose the right environment.** Ensure you sit in a quiet place, avoid backlighting, elevate the camera to eye level, and prevent others from interrupting the session.
- **Show up optimally.** Consider to have your video camera turned on during the sessions, but to keep their audio on "mute" unless it is their turn to speak. The use of headphones is also encouraged.
- **Schedule securely** Mark all sessions in their calendars and, if necessary, set a reminder. The course facilitator might send you reminders and, if the group is run online, the link to meet up each week.

Self-care

As we are about to start with the writing practices, we want to remind you to take care of yourself as much as possible. What do we mean by this? We mean that your writings, being drafts and not stories written on stone, can be edited, nuanced, and transformed. You get to choose what to write, when to write it, and how much of it to share with your peer-support group, your counselor, your family members, friends, and on your social media. Being listened to with compassion is healing, however, there is a time and place for sharing. It's important to acknowledge your vulnerability in sharing and to share only in a way that feels safe. When we facilitate the groups of therapeutic writing, one of our core premises is to respect the emotional rhythms (i.e., tempo and shifting moods) of one another, to develop safety and respect so that we can honor the stories of grief and, in doing so, honor you and your child. Taking care of yourself means listening to yourself, being honest with yourself as you write, and reaching out for support.

Chapter 1

A tale of three stories

Weekly theme(s): Hope, grief and therapeutic writing.

Estimated time: 3 hours, including two pauses of 10 minutes each.

Embracing compassion: You might be both looking forward to working on grief, and resistant or scared about it. It can be terrifying for many of us to get in touch with our pain and our narratives of the loss. Bear with the process and listen to grief at your own rhythm.

Gentle reminder: We calculated the timeframes and the intensity that we indicate for each assignment based on our experiences facilitating several online groups of therapeutic writing. In case you are using this workbook on your own, without the support of a facilitator or a group, it is essential that you listen to your own emotional rhythm and write at your own pace. Take pauses when necessary and, ideally, use this workbook together with someone, be it a peer, a counselor, or a clinician. Check our suggestions on page 2-4.

DOI: 10.4324/9781003423270-2

Guidelines for Group Practice

If using this workbook as part of a writing group, you will have an opportunity to introduce yourself.

Part 1

🕐 Estimated time: 8 minutes

You will be working in dyads in the room, or in a break-out room if online.
Each person has 4 minutes to share the following information:

1 First name + city.
2 The name of the child you want to remember during the course.
3 What motivated you to sign up for the course?
4 What expectations/concerns you may have?

NOTE:

- You don't need to tell the whole story of your loss when introducing yourself in these four minutes, which is certainly a short time to fully express all you need to say. We will have enough time during the course to focus on your story. For the time being, stick to the four points mentioned above.
- We suggest the person who is in the role of listening to another participant to *write down* what they say! Later, when back to whole group, you will introduce each other to the rest of the group.

Part 2

🕐 Estimated time: 20 minutes.

Back to the whole group, each participant will introduce the other person they worked with in the break-out rooms.

1 First name of your classmate, and first name of the child they have lost.
2 Shortly said, what motivated them to sign up for the course?

1.1 Warm-up

1.1.1 Meditative writing

🕐 Estimated time: 5 minutes

Guidelines for Group Practice

If you are using this workbook as part of a writing group in an online setting, you can turn off your camera while you write, if you feel it will help you to be more present in your reflections. The facilitator will let you know when is a minute left before returning to the whole group, and then you can turn your camera on again.

🔊 In case you want to listen to this meditation, follow this link to find a recording.

For the next few minutes, bring your awareness inward, step by step.

Notice first your surroundings and briefly write about them. Describe the physical place where you are right now, as you transition into writing practice. Are there any colors, shapes, or objects that call your attention? Do you notice any smell, sound, or texture?

_____

_____

_____

_____

Now, when you are ready, bring your attention to your body as it sits wherever you are. What parts of your body are in contact with the chair/floor? How do you know that your body is in contact with the chair/floor? Are there any physical sensations you can notice, such as warmth, coolness, a tingling sensation, or even discomfort?

Write down what you notice.

_____

_____

_____

_____

Is there something you need to do to feel more comfortable as you sit here today?

_____

_____

_____

_____

Now, bring your attention inwards, and list the thoughts that pass through or spin around in your mind. Are there any worries, concerns, images, or memories that arise?

_____

_____

_____

Notice if there are any emotions present for you right now. At times, it is easier to notice what we "don't feel" than to know what we feel! It is also okay if today you feel rather numb or quiet. Thus, write down any emotion that is dominant, absent, or name the numbness or quietness. For writing, all you need is to begin wherever you are.

_____

_____

_____

_____

Now, set one or two intentions for today's practice. Examples of such intentions are as follows:

General intentions when writing

- To be as present as possible during today's session.
- To feel closer to my child as I write.
- To tolerate uncomfortable emotions that can arise during the session.
- To take care of myself, and write at my own pace today, even if this means to take a pause from writing.
- To create something raw, honest, and or beautiful.
- Fill in this space with another intention if you find a personal one that is not mentioned above.

_____

_____

_____

_____

Specific intentions targeting the topics for this week

- To hope to feel better, or to hope for something else.
- To be open toward a feeling of hope, even if right now I do not feel a strong sense of hope.
- If you have another personal intention that you want to have in focus for this week, write it down….

_____

_____

_____

_____

My intention for this week's practice is:

_____

_____

_____

_____

1.1.2 Check-in

Estimated time: 4–6 minutes

Sometimes we think that we do not have a right to feel certain ways about loss, or about our struggles to go about everyday life activities, this course included. This check-in is an opportunity for you to have an honest dialogue with yourself, as well as an opportunity to allow yourself to feel whatever you are feeling with compassion and acceptance. We will do this check-in each week, so you can have an overview of what you notice and learn about your emotional world throughout the course.

Give yourself a chance to fill in the first words that arise in your stream of consciousness. There are no right or wrong ways to feel, so do not think too much over the answer, and let words come to you with as little judgment as possible.

Throughout this program of therapeutic writing, all feelings are welcome because being aware and turning toward those feelings with curiosity and compassion will guide you in finding the themes, scenes, and lines in your writings. We are expecting that, at times, it will be difficult to find a word that is accurate enough about the way you feel and therefore we have also made a table (Table 1.1) that can serve you as inspiration to fill in the blanks for this practice.

- I feel _____ and
_____ about my grief today.
- I don't feel _____ and
_____ about my grief today.
- Today I feel, _____ and
_____ about the writing course.
- Today I DON'T feel, _____ and
_____ about the writing course.

Table 1.1 Suggestions for emotions for the weekly check-in practice

Possible emotions				*Other emotions not present in the list (please add)*
Adaptable	Confused	Jealous	Peaceful	
Agitated	Critical	Joyful	Pensive	
Alienated	Content	Light	Pessimistic	
Afraid	Curious	Loving	Positive	
Angry	Distressed	Lonely	Relaxed	
Annoyed	Disturbed	Mad	Relieved	
Anxious	Empty	Melancholic	Resistant	
Apathetic	Euphoric	Miserable	Sad	
Ashamed	Excited	Mixed up	Safe	
Brave	Frustrated	Motivated	Serene	
Bitter	Gloomy	Mortified	Skeptical	
Bored	Grateful	Moody	Strong	
Bittersweet	Guilty/ Remorseful	Nauseated	Uncertain	
Calm	Happy	Negative	Unhappy	
Caring	Hopeful	Nostalgic	Vibrant	
Cautious	Humiliated	Numb	Vulnerable	
Chaotic	Humbled	Optimistic	Worried	
Confident	Infuriated	Outside of myself	Weak	
Comfortable	Inspired	Overwhelmed	Wonderful	

Note: The list of emotions suggested in this table is inspired by the overview of emotional categories in English available at The Berkeley Well-being Institute (Davis, n.d.), the Multiple Affect Adjective Checklist (Gotlib & Meyer, 1986), our clinical experience, and other words that our participants have used to describe their experiences.

Learning Some Theory Together

Estimated time: 10 minutes

I-as-an-author of my grief story

If we observe ourselves closely, we notice that our mind is wired for dialogue and that these dialogues occur not only with other persons but also with inner characters that exist in our inner world, as when we imagine what we will say to a friend, or how our friend might respond. At other times, we could go back and forth about a decision about which we are ambivalent, trying to convince ourselves of one position or another. At still other points, we might hear the voice of a parent or judge criticizing us for a real or imagined failing. In this chapter, we draw inspiration from Huber Hermans's Dialogical Self Theory (Hermans, Kempen & Van Loon, 1992; Hermans, 2001), which we will expand upon in Chapter 3 of this workbook.

For the time being, consider your mind as if it were a theater or a film set, where there are different characters forming your identity. These characters have diverse attitudes, habits, and values, so it is not surprising that from time to time you find yourself experiencing tension because there are contradictory feelings, thoughts, and intentions within. You can be a griever and feel overwhelmed by the intensity of feelings regarding the death of your son or daughter. You might also be a mother or father of a living child, a partner or a single person, a daughter or son, an employee, a student, a leader, or a friend. You can also be the person who has certain hobbies and has decided to build or craft something to honor your child. All these parts of you belong to the person you are as a whole. This is helpful to recognize, as different "parts" or aspects of you bring different needs and resources to the process of grieving your child and adapting to a changed future.

You can also take a meta-perspective and consider yourself as the *author* of your grief story as you engage in these practices of therapeutic writing. Which aspects of your identity seem more present right now, and who might you become as the author of your story? This question will help you zoom into the feelings, emotions, images, and memories that arise, as well as zooming out to reflect upon them, understand your attitudes, needs, and desires.

Three layers of meaning in your grief story

Throughout the years we have worked closely with bereaved families in collaboration with LUB and have developed a threefold frame to guide you during this writing course. We invite you to imagine that there are three layers of meaning in the stories you are to write, and as you edit them you hold space for grief. The first of them is the story *you might want to tell* someone. The second story is that *you need to tell*. For some these two stories might be the same, while for others there is a difference between what they want to narrate and what they need to narrate. The third story is the one other people in similar situations *could learn from* – that is, the story that might accompany and inspire others who are going through struggles similar to yours.

The first layer of the grief story, the story that you might want to tell someone, can be quite censored. As you try to make sense of the chaos of your experience, you might feel that you need to adapt to the expectations of others, or that if you were to disclose too much about how you feel, others would judge you or would not understand. This story might also reflect a mask or façade you have shown the world as you deal with the overwhelming experience, perhaps in an effort to not "trigger" your partner or other family members dealing with difficult feelings of their own. Or you might want to "move on" and "overcome" grief but such a sense of recovery appears to be far away, or impossible to reach. In the very context of this writing course, many participants feel inclined, at first, to write the story they think the facilitator and or the other group members want to hear, instead of writing the story that is in their hearts, waiting to find voice. We encourage you to note whenever you feel like you need to answer the assignments as a "good student" would do. What is much more important is that you write in a way that feels genuine, and that demands great courage, patience, and honesty from your side.

The second layer of the grief story is the one you need to tell; the one you may have kept to yourself and held in silence, perhaps for a long time. You may find that the story that you write at this stage is raw. As you dare to open this inner room to express what you feel compelled to say, oftentimes you may feel conflicted or afraid. The story you need to tell could involve a deep sense of vulnerability and fragility, as well as the humility to recognize where you are stuck, and where you might need support from others. This story situates grief in the context of your biography and gives an account of how grief might at times amplify the pain of past emotional injuries, losses, and traumas. Many people feel a shift to greater insight and understanding when they shift from the story of how grief is shaping their life, to the story of how their life is shaping the way they grieve.

The third layer of your grief story opens the possibility to put your suffering into service, to offer a story that other people who are struggling can use as an inspiration as they find their own way through life challenges. This story embraces the fruits of finding meaning through and despite the death of your child. This layer of narration turns your story of grief into a lighthouse that can accompany them as they live and experience the darkness of despair inherent to grief. Discovering or writing this story will take time, and it usually follows the first two, as we gradually find nuggets of meaning in the mourning despite the pain it brings in its wake.

The challenge is to engage these layers of meaning within your grief story through writing that is both genuine and gentle. Neither forcing yourself to write what you feel *others* want to hear nor writing what you think you *should* feel and think instead of what you *do* feel and think will help much in this process. It is in crossing the threshold into candor with yourself that emotional processing and integration take place.

Now, let's get started!

1.2 PRACTICE: Becoming an author of your grief story

1.2.1 Writing my own storylines

Estimated time: 4–6 minutes

Considering your identity as a complex cast of characters, answer the following questions:

- If your mind were a theater or a film set, which parts of yourself seem more active and quiet at the time being?

_____

_____

_____

_____

- What motivates you to explore therapeutic writing?

_____

_____

_____

_____

- What are your expectations from these practices?

_____

_____

_____

_____

- Do you have any concerns, worries, or experiences you hope to avoid?

_____

_____

_____

_____

1.2.2 Using literature as inspiration

Estimated time: 3 minutes

Read the following poem out loud:

Hope

Hi, hope,
you, twining yourself in between the roots,
covered in moss and autumn softness,
your warm breath on my neck.

Hi, hope!
Hi, there in the in-between spaces,
lovingly whispering from the other side
of all the things we deem impossible, hi!
Here we are, here we come!

Hi!

(Åsmund Seip, 2019, p. 25, translated by
Olga Lehmann & Åsmund Seip)

Highlight a sentence that caught your attention in this poem. Do so intuitively, based on words that captivated your attention for one or another reason. Try not to overthink, as there are no right or wrong stanzas in the poem.

1.2.3 Time to take perspective

🕒 Estimated time: 5 minutes

How do you feel about hope within grief today? Use the sentence you highlighted in the poem as a part of your answer.

_____

_____

_____

_____

_____

1.3 PRACTICE: Listening to music as we listen to ourselves

1.3.1 Listening to music as you write

🕒 Estimated time: 20 minutes

Many of the bereaved parents we have worked with tell us that there are songs dear to their hearts because they have played them at the funeral, because the music expresses their grief, because it reminds them of their child, or because it seems particularly consoling for them. These may be lyrical or instrumental compositions, and they may play them at home, when driving, on a walk, or even when writing. These parents have found comfort or meaning in music, as well as the possibility to lean into the melancholy, the longings, and the rage, which are at times unbearable and unspeakable. Music has been the writing companion for many writers, both in the case of published authors and in the case of most of us who write because we want to process difficult emotions and find meaning through life tragedies.

In the field of therapeutic writing, there are different methods that rely on music, such as general creative explorations with unfamiliar music as prompts (Edwards, 2017), or more specific methods such as the "Music Chronology" (Duffey, 2007), or "Proprioceptive Writing" (Metcalf & Simon, 2002), which simply means writing that helps us _perceive ourselves_ with greater clarity.

For this practice, we want you to listen to a piece of instrumental music, either it is a baroque piece, as suggested by Metcalf and Simon (2002). We generally discourage participants from actively listening to songs with lyrics for this very writing practice, as these seem to overly dictate or constrain the content to follow. However, we do encourage participants to think of songs that have been meaningful to them throughout life, similarly to Duffey (2007), as these songs can be rich in metaphors, memories, and forms of expression that can supplement the further development of writings, and the integration of grief into their lives.

◁)))) **Suggestions for Users**

As for music suggestions, we encourage you to listen, for example, to composers such as Bach, Handel, or Vivaldi. If you want to experiment with contemporary music, we have had positive experiences with, for example, the Italian composer Ludovico Einaudi, or popular performers of reflective instrumental music, such as David Lantz or Mia Jang. We have also created a Spotify list Music for writing with some suggestions. This is the link:

https://open.spotify.com/playlist/6Rb8NseLxosZ9hjmGsYWVs?si=xfN82kvvSQ-cAlhkCa1lTg

Feel free to use it as inspiration and to add tracks that seem to help you.

In the online writing courses that we have facilitated we have had positive results when we encourage participants to listen to instrumental music as mindfully as they can for about 5–7 minutes, and once the piece is over, to write for 10 minutes about what they need to say, inspired by the song. Some participants would prefer to write bullet points or words as they listen to the song and elaborate about them afterward. Others prefer to first turn their attention to the music, and then write about it after the song has ended. Either way is fine, so do what suits you best as you listen! Whatever you decide works best for you, follow these guidelines, inspired by some of the instructions in the Proprioceptive Method (Metcalf & Simon, 2002) that we have adapted throughout the development of this writing course:

1 **Writing down what we notice within.** This is a practice of connecting with the immediacy of what is happening to us. Write whatever you become aware of – either the images, feelings, thoughts, and memories that arise or perceptions about listening to the music itself. Remain curious and ask yourself: *what do I notice, right now?*
2 **Have an honest conversation with yourself.** Either because of perfectionism, self-criticism, fear of being judged, or shame for what we think, feel, or do, we tend to interrupt ourselves when we speak, and when we write. Try, as best as you can, not to censor yourself in this practice, as there is no right or wrong way to feel grief, and the acceptance of whatever happens in our inner world is often healing.
3 **Observe what we are writing.** Attend to the words that are being written, even if they are painful to recognize at first. Aim at using writing as an opportunity to have an honest conversation with yourself and learn more about what you need and want at the time being.
4 **Ask yourself and answer the proprioceptive question.** This form of writing encourages us to both connect with the music and let words find their way onto the paper and then take perspective on what is being disclosed. The latter step happens when we ask the so-called proprioceptive question, "What do I mean by…?" and write its consequent answer, "What I mean by _____ is…." (Metcalf & Simon, 2002). Together, these simple but subtle question/answer sequences support the process of meaning-making. For instance, this proprioceptive question could look like:

My mother was always talking as she knitted. What do I mean by "talking"? By talking I mean that she would have a loud conversation with herself. It was her own ritual to deal with the chaos at home. What do I mean by chaos? By chaos I mean that everyone would be running through the living room after dinner if dessert was not served.

If you want to learn more about the method in its traditional form, we recommend the book *Writing the Mind Alive. The Proprioceptive Method for Finding Your Authentic Voice*, by Metcalf and Simon (2002).

Use the proprioceptive questions as many times as you find it necessary as you write. Focus your question on keywords that nonetheless seem ambiguous, as a way of clarifying and deepening the writing. Answering this question will help you describe situations and your responses to them more in detail and ensure that you write down what you are listening to as much as you are listening to what you are writing. Think about this question as a tool for being grounded in the moment as you put your experiences into words.

As part of the process, it is important to write without thinking too much about the grammar or logic of the writing, for instance.

Now, write following the three steps explained above, ideally as you listen or after you have listened to the instrumental music of your choice:

_____

_____

_____

_____

_____

_____

_____

_____

_____

_____

_____

_____

_____

_____

_____

_____

_____

_____

_____

_____

_____

_____

1.3.2   *Time to take perspective*

🕐 Estimated time: 5 minutes

Metcalf and Simon (2002) suggest that proprioceptive writing should be followed by some time for reflecting on the process. We have modified some of the questions they suggest and added some others below that our writing group members have found helpful. We encourage you to spend a few minutes answering them as spontaneously and genuinely as you can.

How or what do you feel now after the writing practice?

_____

_____

_____

_____

Did anything surprising or interesting arise for you in this writing? If so, what was it about?

_____

_____

_____

_____

What thoughts, feelings, images, physical sensations, did you notice but, for one or another reason, decided not to write down?

_____

_____

_____

_____

What could have been the possible reason for not writing some of these experiences down in the first take of the practice?

_____

_____

_____

_____

How was the music for you? Is there any other song you would consider using as an inspiration for writing?

_____

_____

_____

_____

1.3.3   What did you notice?

🕒 Estimated time: 5 minutes

Now that you have had the experience of writing with music as a companion, and reflected about it, what do you notice about yourself? For example, how easy or difficult was it to get started and write?

_____

_____

_____

_____

What thoughts, emotions, physical sensations in the body, images, or memories emerge right now, as you zoom out to look at the experience?

_____

_____

_____

_____

Is there any popular song whose lyrics represent some of what you feel or experience? If so, which one?

_____

_____

_____

_____

Guidelines for Group Practice

🕐 Estimated time: 15 minutes

If you are using this workbook as part of a writing group, pair with another participant and share what you noticed in response to the reflective questions that interest you. Then, after 10 minutes to do so, go back into the whole group where people will have an opportunity to, voluntarily, share what they noticed in their paired conversations, focusing on their own contributions for about 5 minutes.

   This practice is mainly about sharing how members experienced the writing practice. You do not need to share what you wrote!

Learning Some Theory Together

🕐 Estimated time: 10 minutes

Therapeutic writing in a nutshell

Throughout history, human beings have mastered language and writing practices as a form of connecting with others for the purpose of coordinating their actions, negotiating differences, teaching and learning, and simply sharing experiences. Especially when it focused on difficult experiences, writing undoubtedly had beneficial effects long before psychologists reflected on it and provided evidence of its benefits.

   For writing to be therapeutic, it needs to do more than merely describing external events. Just focusing on "what happened" can lead to rumination, overthinking, and the activation of difficult emotions (Pennebaker & Smyth, 2016). What you need to do in addition to describing what happened is to "time travel with emotion," making a genuine attempt to find words for whatever arose for you, in the difficult moment you are describing, what you are feeling now as you write, and how you imagine you might feel in the future. This shift of focus to your feelings and emotions can help you not only make more sense of what happened but also to make more sense of yourself and your emotions in light of it.

Another way of saying this is that as you shift from the external, more or less objective story to the internal, emotion-focused story, you begin to engage the deeper themes of the meaning-oriented story, to discover its larger significance, in a way that shapes your values and purpose (Neimeyer, 1999; Lehmann et al., 2022). Some questions that can help you in the process of writing can be: What did I feel back then? What do I feel right now as we write about it? How do I want to feel in the future? (Lichtenthal & Neimeyer, 2012).

Similarly, we might want to write about how our experiences of values such as gratitude, friendship, hope, or compassion change through time. Many participants we have worked with have experiences of resistance, tension, ambiguity, and ambivalence. Also, write about that! Part of this process might involve remembering how you felt during the days close to the death of your child. Doing so might be uncomfortable, although it will also help you heal, as you find words for these emotions. We encourage you to trust that whatever feelings emerge as you write, they are important and require your attention, care, and compassion.

Once you embark on your writing journey you are likely to find yourself reflecting on other aspects of your life story. Remember, as an author of your story, be committed to honesty. Instead of being a "good student" or imagining what others are expecting from you – such as your family, a group facilitator, or a peer, write about your experiences as they are, and your path of becoming. This makes post-traumatic growth possible. One way to notice the therapeutic effects of doing so would be to discover a transition between a first version of the story, often vulnerable accounts of suffering in which you appear to be stuck, and a second version of the story that feels more engaged with the life that is, despite the tragedy (Lengelle & Meijers, 2009).

In addition, remember that even if you might feel alone as you transit the darkness of grief, YOU ARE NOT ALONE! There are different support systems available such as family and friends, peer-support and volunteer organizations, counseling, and specialized healthcare in the public or private sector. If you are engaged in a writing group of other bereaved parents, they may prove to be among your most important fellow travelers.

Have this in mind when writing

Writing can be helpful and painful at the same time. Research findings indicate that in the short term, people who write about challenging experiences can experience distress and or anxiety; however, in the long-term perspective, the benefits of writing override the temporary discomfort (e.g., Pennebaker, 1993). In the world of psychotherapy and trauma, we often speak about working within our "window of tolerance" (Corrigan et al., 2011). Working within your window of tolerance means that you have a unique threshold for how much suffering you can deal with at a given moment and that you also react, consciously or not, differently when your tender spots are triggered. Some of these reactions involve, for example, a sense of numbness, avoidance, or acting out of rage. Therefore, we encourage you to approach your suffering and vulnerability gently, taking pauses from writing if necessary, especially if you are following this workbook on your own, without support from a group or a facilitator. We also offer guidelines for how to write in a safely tolerable way about difficult topics – the surest way to develop more mastery of your grief and even learn from it (see page 2-4).

1.4   PRACTICE: Chapters of our lives

1.4.1   *Writing your autobiography*

🕐 Estimated time: 12 minutes

This is an adaptation of a technique developed by Robert Neimeyer (2014), and widely used in grief therapy.

Imagine you are 95 years old and are writing your memoir or autobiography at this point in your life. What would the Table of Contents look like? What would be the titles for each of its chapters? Write the titles of chapters that capture the whole arc of your life, the good and bad of it. If possible, go beyond standard lists of life stages (Birth, Infancy, Childhood, School Years, University, Work, Marriage, Parenting, etc.) to capture in images, metaphors, or language that is right for you something about that period or chapter that captures its essence for you (A Star is Born, Growing Up Alone, Darkness Visible, A New Hope, What's Love Got to Do with It?, etc.). You can create the titles for these chapters in any way that feels best for you, whether or not the content would be immediately apparent to another reader. There are no right nor wrong ways to do this, as this is just the first draft for such a table of contents. Draft as many chapter titles as you like to acknowledge the different episodes that are important in your life story.

Don't overthink as you write, and start from the point in time that feels the most relevant for you.

Table of contents

The Chapters of My Life

1.

2.

3.

4. (etc.)

_____

_____

_____

_____

_____

_____

_____

_____

1.4.2   Time to take perspective

🕐 Estimated time: 12 minutes

Now that you have written down your first draft of the chapters of your life, reflect in writing on these follow-up questions. We encourage you to answer <u>at least four</u> of them, those that appeal to you the most. Of course, as further homework, you might choose to reflect on more of the questions, of all of them!

Organization

- When would the book of your life start according to this table of contents?
- How did you organize the flow of this autobiography? By years, or in some other way?

Development

- As you look back on how your life story has developed over time, do the changes appear gradually, or are they more revolutionary and sudden?
- How did you decide when one chapter ended and a new one began?
- What role, if any, did significant loss experiences (deaths, relationship breakups, moving to new homes, serious illness of self or a family member, loss of job) play in marking such transitions?

Themes

- Looking at the story, what are the major themes that tie it together, such as themes of abandonment, love, problem solving, new beginnings?
- Do you notice any minor themes that pull in a different direction? If so, how might the story be different if they were really to have their say?

Authorship

- Who do you see as the primary author of this self-narrative? Are there any important co-authors who deserve credit (or blame!) for the way the story has unfolded?
- How might your chapters have looked different if they had been formulated from the standpoint of the person you were 10 years ago?
- Who would you most trust to write your autobiography if you could not? Who would you definitely not want to "hand the pen" to?

Audience

- Who is the most relevant audience for this book? Who would enjoy the way it is written, and who would want to "edit" it?
- Are there any "silent stories" in your life that have no audience, that cannot be told? (Remember that you need not share anything you write with others.)
- How would your life be different if these silent stories were included in the public story shared with others?

Framing

- Where on the shelves of a library could this book be placed? Would it be a comedy, tragedy, history, mystery, adventure story, or romance? Or would different chapters represent "short stories" of different kinds? If so, which of them would you like to expand?
- If this story of your life had a sequel or second volume, what might it be entitled?

Write down your selection of the questions above and answer them.

_____

_____

_____

_____

_____

_____

_____

_____

_____

_____

_____

_____

_____

_____

_____

_____

_____

_____

_____

_____

_____

_____

1.4.3   What did you notice?

🕐 Estimated time: 8 minutes

What did you notice when writing during this practice?

_____

_____

_____

_____

If you were to project a future new chapter beyond the present moment, perhaps capturing changes in your life in the next 5 years, what might that chapter be titled? What could be the value of envisioning this chapter as you seek to both *live with* and *live beyond* your loss?

_____

_____

_____

_____

In what ways might the story of your life be larger than the loss of your child? And what meaning would you want your child's brief life to have in the larger structure of your life story?

_____

_____

_____

_____

Guidelines for Group Practice

🕐 Estimated time: 15 minutes

If you are using this workbook as part of a writing group, pair with another participant and share what you noticed in response to the reflective questions that interest you. Then, after 10 minutes to do so, go back into the whole group where people will have an opportunity to, voluntarily, share what they noticed in their paired conversations, focusing on their own contributions.

This practice is mainly about sharing how members experienced the writing practice. You do not need to share what you wrote!

1.5   Check out journaling

Estimated time: 4 minutes

Now that you are finishing this chapter, use some minutes to answer the following questions, without thinking too much about what you are to write. Answer in a way that feels spontaneous and genuine for you.

What have I learned about grief today?

_____

_____

_____

What have I learned about writing today?

_____

_____

_____

What have I learned about myself today?

_____

_____

_____

1.6   Further practice

1.6.1   *Practicing the listening to music as you write*

Estimated time: 8–12 minutes

Listen to your favorite instrumental song (i.e., without lyrics) – or the song we used in class while practicing Proprioceptive Writing for at least 5 minutes. Use the reflection questions in (PAGE 17) to look back at your writing.

_____

_____

_____

_____

_____

_____

_____

_____

_____

_____

_____

_____

_____

_____

_____

_____

_____

_____

_____

_____

_____

_____

_____

1.6.2 *Time to take perspective*

Estimated time: 5 minutes

Which emotions (if any) appear in this writing?

_____

_____

_____

_____

How can you connect whatever you wrote with hope (e.g., the experience of hope, the need for hope, the desire to have hope, or moments of hopelessness)?

_____

_____

_____

_____

_____

_____

Use the poem by Åsmund Seip (PAGE 15) for inspiration.

Guidelines for Group Practice

If you are using this workbook as part of a writing group, whether online or onsite, you will have a chance to share about this practice at the beginning of the next class.

Chapter 2

What am I resisting?

Weekly theme(s): Resistance as a part of grief.

Estimated time: 2.5 hours, including two pauses of 10 minutes each.

Embracing compassion: You might both look forward to writing and feel afraid about what it will involve. As much as people want to work on their grief, it might be terrifying for many of us to get in touch with our pain and our narratives of the loss. You are the expert about your own life story, and it is important to be in contact with your thoughts, memories, emotions, images, and physical sensations in the body at your own rhythm.

Gentle reminder: We calculated the timeframes and the intensity that we indicate for each assignment based on our experiences facilitating online groups of therapeutic writing. In case you are using this workbook on your own, without the support of a facilitator or a group, it is essential that you listen to your own emotional rhythm and write at your own pace. Take pauses when necessary and, ideally, use this workbook together with someone, be it a peer, a counselor, or a clinician. Check our suggestions on page 2-4.

DOI: 10.4324/9781003423270-3

2.1 Warm-up

2.1.1 *Meditative writing*

Estimated time: 5 minutes

Guidelines for Group Practice

If you are using this workbook as part of a writing group in an online setting, you can turn off your camera while you write, if you feel it will help you to be more present in your reflections. The facilitator will let you know when is a minute left before returning to the whole group, and then you can turn your camera on again.

In case you want to listen to this meditation, follow this link to find a recording.

For the next few minutes, bring your awareness inward, step by step.

Notice first your surroundings and briefly write about them. Describe the physical place where you are right now, as you transition into writing practice. Are there any colors, shapes, or objects that call your attention? Do you notice any smell, sound, or texture?

_____

_____

_____

Now, when you are ready, bring your attention to your body as it sits wherever you are. What parts of your body are in contact with the chair/floor? How do you know that your body is in contact with the chair/floor? Are there any physical sensations you can notice, such as warmth, coolness, a tingling sensation, or even discomfort?

Write down what you notice.

_____

_____

_____

Is there something you need to do to feel more comfortable as you sit here today?

_____

_____

_____

_____

Now, bring your attention inwards, and list the thoughts that pass through or spin around in your mind. Are there any worries, concerns, images, or memories that arise?

_____

_____

_____

_____

Notice if there are any emotions present for you right now. At times, it is easier to notice what we "don't feel" than to know what we feel! It is also okay if today you feel rather numb or quiet. Thus, write down any emotion that is dominant, absent, or name the numbness or quietness. For writing, all you need is to begin wherever you are.

_____

_____

_____

_____

Now, set one or two intentions for today's practice. Examples of such intentions are as follows:

General intentions when writing

- To be as present as possible during today's session
- To feel closer to my child as I write
- To tolerate uncomfortable emotions that can arise during the session
- To take care of myself, and write at my own pace today, even if this means to take a pause from writing.
- To create something raw, honest, and or beautiful
- Fill in this space with another intention if you find a personal one that is not mentioned above.

_____

_____

_____

_____

Specific intentions to the week's theme

- To be curious about the ways in which resistance to grief shows up today, instead of judging it or avoiding uncomfortable feelings.
- To trust that resistance is a natural part of grieving and that focusing on it explicitly will be helpful for my process.

- To notice the parts of my feeling of resistance that are healthy, and that help me to put energy into aspects of life other than grief.
- If you have another personal intention that you want to have in focus for this week, write it down…

_____

_____

_____

_____

My intention for this week's practice is:

_____

_____

_____

_____

_____

2.1.2 Check-in

Estimated time: 4 minutes

Sometimes we think that we do not have a right to feel certain ways about loss, or about our struggles to go about everyday life activities, this course included. This check-in is an opportunity for you to have an honest dialogue with yourself, as well as an opportunity to allow yourself to feel whatever you are feeling with compassion and acceptance. We will do this check-in each week, so you can have an overview of what you notice and learn about your emotional world throughout the course.

Give yourself a chance to fill in the first words that arise in your stream of consciousness. There are no right or wrong ways to feel, so do not think too much over the answer, and let words come to you with as little judgment as possible.

Throughout this program of therapeutic writing, all feelings are welcome because being aware and turning toward those feelings with curiosity and compassion will guide you in finding the themes, scenes, and lines in your writings. We are expecting that, at times, it will be difficult to find a word that is accurate enough about the way you feel and therefore we have also made a table (Table 2.1) that can serve you as inspiration to fill in the blanks for this practice.

- I feel _____ and _____ about my grief today.
- I don't feel _____ and _____ about my grief today.
- Today I feel, _____ and _____ about the writing course.
- Today I DON'T feel, _____ and _____ about the writing course.

Table 2.1 Suggestions for emotions for the weekly check-in practice

Possible emotions				Other emotions not present in the list (please add)
Adaptable	Confused	Jealous	Peaceful	
Agitated	Critical	Joyful	Pensive	
Alienated	Content	Light	Pessimistic	
Afraid	Curious	Loving	Positive	
Angry	Distressed	Lonely	Relaxed	
Annoyed	Disturbed	Mad	Relieved	
Anxious	Empty	Melancholic	Resistant	
Apathetic	Euphoric	Miserable	Sad	
Ashamed	Excited	Mixed up	Safe	
Brave	Frustrated	Motivated	Serene	
Bitter	Gloomy	Mortified	Skeptical	
Bored	Grateful	Moody	Strong	
Bittersweet	Guilty/ Remorseful	Nauseated	Uncertain	
Calm	Happy	Negative	Unhappy	
Caring	Hopeful	Nostalgic	Vibrant	
Cautious	Humiliated	Numb	Vulnerable	
Chaotic	Humbled	Optimistic	Worried	
Confident	Infuriated	Outside of myself	Weak	
Comfortable	Inspired	Overwhelmed	Wonderful	

Note: The list of emotions suggested in this table is inspired by the overview of emotional categories in English available at The Berkeley Well-being Institute (Davis, n.d.), the Multiple Affect Adjective Checklist (Gotlib & Meyer, 1986), our clinical experience, and other words that our participants have used to describe their experiences.

2.2 PRACTICE: Reflecting about the home practices

2.2.1 Time to take perspective

🕐 Estimated time: 4 minutes

As you might remember from the introduction, home practices in between sessions are not mandatory. We are, however, curious about your level of motivation toward them.

• If you set a time for writing. What did you notice this week while you tried to write?

_____

_____

_____

_____

- If you did not write in between sessions, what could have possibly held you back from doing so?

_____

_____

_____

_____

- How was this different from how you usually pay attention to your grief?

_____

_____

_____

_____

Guidelines for Group Practice

🕐 Estimated time: 10 minutes

If you are using this workbook as part of a writing group, you will work in pairs and or groups of three–four people, and share your answers to these questions. You will only share what you feel is okay for you to share, as the others will listen without interrupting or refocusing on their own experiences. Each of the participants will have their own turn to share.

Learning Theory Together

🕐 Estimated time: 4–6 minutes

Notes on grief and resistance

Among academic disciplines, there are different theories and perspectives about what grief is, what a natural or complicated course of grief is like, how bereaved people like you experience it, and what is helpful or not for interventions.

Our perspective is that grieving is a process, and not a state you overcome and get rid of. As you find your way, at times relying on the support of others, you will reconcile with the difficult emotions, thoughts, beliefs, memories, and ideas about how your future was supposed to be, as you seek a sense of renewed purpose and meaning in your life. Of course, doing so is extremely challenging. After all, it is in principle paradoxical that you are to find meaning out of meaningless tragedies, such as the death of your child. For this, you have all of our warmest sense of compassion and care, as we have put our hearts, page by page, into giving you a sense of comfort and help.

One popular framework to understand grief nowadays is called the Dual Process Model (Stroebe & Schut, 1999). According to this model, as you go about your everyday life, you are both oriented toward grief with its challenges and opportunities, as well as oriented toward restoring your life despite it, which also implies its own challenges and opportunities. This means that it is important as it is for you to find a balance between being in the "grief space", giving yourself permission to step out of it and engaging in other everyday life activities is essential. It is this pendulum swing between loss and life that can promote self-understanding and compassion about your loss, on the one hand, and a sense of mastery, motivation, or confidence about your ongoing life on the other. In other words, coping with grief in a healthy way demands us to oscillate between focusing on our inner reactions and thoughts and turning our attention outwards and adapting, step by step, to the consequences that the loss gives us (Kristensen, Dyregrov og Dyregrov, 2021).

Many bereaved people experience grief as coming and going in waves that are difficult to control. Suddenly you feel overwhelmed and taken to a dark and daunting place, and you struggle to focus on other things. Thinking about the future with optimism seems unrealistic. At other moments, you seem to find energy or motivation to take care of different tasks at home or at work and manage to move through the days in one or another.

Those days that feel better might well surprise you with instances of joy. Ironically that same joy can also arouse a sense of guilt, perhaps because feeling even flickers of happiness or pleasure betrays the love you have for your child or your grief over such a loss. But the reality is that a great range of emotions spontaneously arise in the course of bereavement and are to be welcomed as having a part to play in your adaptation to a changed world. You might also feel rage, regret, jealousy, shame, guilt, despair, and many more emotions, alongside gratitude, love, pride, and hope. This is one reason we have built the check-in practices into the various chapters, to give you an opportunity to find accurate words to describe what you are feeling, even when these emotions come in complex or contradictory tangles that need to be teased apart patiently.

On the one hand, the *loss orientation* in the Dual Process Model involves your intention to make sense of the death of your beloved one, and navigate the difficult emotions and moods related to it (Stroebe & Schut, 2010). Intrusive waves of grief may take over, or you may miss an opportunity to focus on other dimensions of life and the future. On the other hand, a *restoration* orientation implies a call to attend to different life challenges and tasks unrelated to the grief *(Stroebe & Schut, 2010)*. This can be, among others, engaging in new hobbies such as writing, volunteering, painting, carpentry, or a sport, as well as the basic day-to-day maintenance activities of marketing, preparing meals, running errands, and so on required for our simple survival and that of our families. Finding some ways to be distracted can help you "take a breather" from your grief, as you "relearn the world" and a new way of embracing your identity and the roles you have in life.

Over-engaging in only one side of the dual processes of grief can lead to complications, as avoidance of loss and avoidance of life both come with costs. In the former case, as you write about your personal experiences of grief, you might notice that resistance arises in different forms. Perhaps there is a part of yourself thinking that writing isn't helpful, or that it is better to close this book immediately and permanently. Perhaps you feel tired, anxious, or skeptical as you are about to start writing. Perhaps you find yourself in front of a blank page and feel that no words arise, that there are not enough words, or a right language for the intensity and the chaos of your experiences. Perhaps you feel the urge to do something else, like organizing the kitchen, or having a drink, or laying down and crying. Perhaps, as you think about your next scheduled writing, you feel tempted to skip it and prioritize other things.

Resistance has different shapes and shades. Turning toward it with curiosity can help you pace the changes that are happening in your emotional world. Strive for balance, neither pushing yourself too much or too little. It might be relieving to feel less alone with your suffering to find words for the pain, as most of the families we have worked with would say.

Beware if you sense self-criticism for not writing something beautiful enough, or shame about whatever it is you are acknowledging.

You might feel a strong need to be understood, and to find words to something so dark and difficult. But focusing not only on your experiences of grief and loss but also on the creative aspects of writing can be an ally.

Oscillating between an orientation to grief and an orientation to restoration can be exhausting and at times you can feel lost, or pressured, or even guilty for not "moving on" at a faster pace. You deserve credit for simply writing anything, even if it is a list of words that feel random to begin with. Any raw sketch has potential and you are not alone in finding the process of editing a text exhausting or confusing at times.

When we pick up a published book from a shelf, we are looking at the outcome of years of work and several rounds of editing. In the case of this writing program, we encourage you to adopt a different standard. You do not even need to rationally comprehend what you write at the point of sketching your initial drafts. The most important thing for the time being is that what you write feels genuine, and that you are as honest with yourself as you can be.

We encourage you to consider the writing as a process or tension in moving between who you were at the time of the death of your beloved one, the person you are right now as you write, and the person you are becoming. Grief shapes our sense of identity and invites us to rediscover ourselves, which can be a painful but ultimately inspiring process.

2.3 PRACTICE: A poem for my child

2.3.1 Writing an acrostic with the letters of the name of your child

Estimated time: 10 minutes

For this writing practice, you will create an acrostic – a special kind of poem using each of the letters of the name of your child as the starting point of a sentence or stanza. For example, if the name of your child was Michael, then you would write a word, phrase, or sentence starting with M, another starting with I, and so on, until you have a line for each of the letters of the child's name. It would look like this:

M...
I ...
C...
H...
A...
E...
L...

If there is a story behind the choice of this name, use it as an inspiration. In case your child did not have an official name, perhaps he or she had a nickname or an expression you used to refer to the baby when you talked with your partner or intimate others (e.g., Sprout, baby boy/girl, little one, sweetheart).

Write your own acrostic below. There are no right or wrong ways to do this. Try as best as you can to write lines that feel genuine, and that speak of your bond with your child. Your wishes, your sorrows, your despair, your questions, your ambivalence… Everything is welcome!

_____

_____

_____

_____

_____

_____

_____

_____

_____

_____

_____

_____

_____

2.3.2 *Time to take perspective*

Estimated time: 5 minutes

Answer to the following question:

What did you notice when writing this acrosticon?

_____

_____

_____

_____

Guidelines for Group Practice

🕐 Estimated time: 15 minutes

If you are facilitating this practice in an online setting, you will work in a dyad or in a group of three participants (breakout rooms if running the groups online). Take turns reading the acrostics to one another. While listening to one another, follow these guidelines:

Assign turns for who will start sharing and who will be the listener(s). Plan also who would have the next turn sharing. Use the rule of "who is to the right is next" if it works for you. The facilitator might help you get on track, noting when 5 minutes have passed or sending an electronic note to online breakout groups, to make sure that each person has the same time for sharing before returning to the whole group. Ideally, you can also assign the time tracking responsibility within the group as well.

Guidelines for the person listening:

- Place your hand on your heart to feel grounded as you listen to the other's poem.
- Hold space for the other, whatever emotions arise. If someone cries, simply allow the tears without needing to lessen them.
- Avoid the urge to jump into the conversation with their own stories, comparisons to their experience, or advice. Instead, this practice is about giving space to the other person to be in contact with themselves. Since they are the experts in their own grief, we need to trust that they will find resources that work for them.
- Once the person is done reading their writing, thank them for their courage and ask, *How do you feel now, after having read this text to us?*

2.4 PRACTICE: Virtual dream stories

2.4.1 *Writing your own virtual dream story*

🕐 Estimated time: 15 minutes

In this practice, you will create a fiction story based on three different kinds of prompts: a situation/setting; a figure/voice; and a symbolic object. This is a method called *Virtual Dream Stories* developed by Doug Smith (Neimeyer et al., 2011), and further refined and researched by Neimeyer and Young-Eisendrath (2014). Like a dream, these brief stories, written in just 8–10 minutes, can engage the power of imagination to transcend conventional reality and represent very real themes in our lives but in surprising ways. Without over-thinking, read through the list in Table 2.2 and choose two elements from each of the three categories that somehow interest you. There are no right or wrong choices!

Table 2.2 Possible writing prompts

Situations/settings	Figures/voices	Symbolic objects
A wasting illness	A wise woman	A red rose
A violent storm	A mysterious stranger	A burning fire
A troubled sea	A booming voice	An ancient chart
An early loss	A choking sob	An ambulance
A long journey	A glowing angel	A strange mask
A secret room	A white dove	An empty bed
A cool brook	A whispering serpent	A closed door
An unearthly light	A wrinkled elder	A wooden coffin
A steep precipice	An overheard song	A naked sculpture
A dark cave	A strong man	A treasure box
An empty house	A talking teddy bear	A broken toy
A dark wood	A voice in the wind	A luminous butterfly
Other (write your own...)	Other (write your own...)	Other (write your own...)

Note: This table is adapted with permission from Neimeyer and Young-Eisendrath (2014, p. 63)

Use these 6 elements, in any way you choose, weaving them into a brief fictional story. Write as spontaneously as you can, without censoring yourself or overthinking. Let your creativity flow freely! Set your timer for 8 minutes. Then, if you are still writing when the timer goes off, give yourself just one more minute to finish it up, or outline the conclusion.

_____

_____

_____

_____

_____

_____

_____

_____

_____

_____

_____

_____

_____

_____

_____

_____

_____

_____

_____

_____

_____

_____

_____

_____

_____

2.4.2 *Time to take perspective*

Estimated time: 15 minutes

Answer to the following questions:

How do I feel right now, after writing this story?

_____

_____

With which of the elements in my story did I most identify? With which did I least identify?

I most identified with the:

_____

_____

I least identified with the:

_____

_____

If the first of these elements had a voice, what would it say or ask to the second? And how would the other respond?

Write this brief dialogue here.

_____

_____

_____

_____

Going back to the element with which you most identified, if it had feelings or emotions, how would it feel, in a word or two or phrase?

_____

If this feeling is part of your experience of grief, write down 3 concrete steps you could take this week to address that feeling in some constructive way. Try to frame these as *behaviors* or *actions*, rather than general attitudes or intentions. For example, if you used the image of a *crying child* in your story, and identified with this figure because of the child's feeling of *loneliness*, then you might plan to take the following steps or actions to address this:

1 explore what I mean by loneliness in my therapeutic writing; *What or who am I missing and why?*
2 reach out to friends or family at a distance by email, text or phone to share something in my life, and inquire about theirs
3 arrange to have coffee or go for a long walk with a friend I have not seen for too long.

You get the idea: use the exercise to prompt relevant action, and then follow through on it.

_____

_____

_____

1_____

2_____

3_____

Guidelines for Group Practice

🕒 Estimated time: 15 minutes

If you are using this workbook as part of a writing group, you will have an opportunity to share your insights and reactions with other group members, either in dyads or groups of three. Then, you will also have an opportunity to, voluntarily, share some of your experiences with the whole group.

2.5 Check out journaling

Estimated time: 4 minutes

Now that you are finishing this chapter, use some minutes to answer the following questions, without thinking too much about what you are to write. Answer in a way that feels spontaneous and genuine for you.

What have I learned about grief today?

_____

_____

_____

What have I learned about writing today?

_____

_____

_____

What have I learned about myself today?

_____

_____

_____

2.6 Further practice

2.6.1 Imagining your grief memoir

Estimated time: 10 minutes

If you were to write a memoir about your loss, what would the first page of the book look like? How would the story begin? Use at least 2 prompts from Table 2.2. (p. 40) as inspiration. If you struggle to find words to start, write about that resistance to finding words then!

_____

_____

_____

_____

_____

_____

_____

_____

_____

_____

_____

_____

_____

_____

_____

_____

_____

_____

_____

_____

_____

_____

_____

_____

_____

2.6.2   *Time to take perspective*

🕐 Estimated time: 4 minutes

Which emotions, if any, would be present in this story?

_____

_____

_____

_____

If this text were to give hope to those who read the book, how would the troubling feelings be transformed over the course of the storytelling?

_____

_____

_____

_____

Chapter 3

Dialogue and self-compassion

Weekly theme(s): Psychoeducation and experiential learning practices about the dialogical self, self-care, and self-compassion.

Estimated time: 2–2.5 hours, including two pauses of 10 minutes each.

Embracing compassion: It is easier said than done to focus on self-care and to be kind to ourselves as we grieve. This week, we invite you to look at your own life, as well as to your interactions with others, through dialogical lenses. What do we mean by that? We encourage you to explore your suffering with curiosity and see if important imaginary conversations with parts of yourselves, with family members, with friends, with your dead child, with health care professionals, would unfold through writing.

Gentle reminder: We calculated the timeframes and the intensity that we indicate for each assignment based on our experiences facilitating online groups of therapeutic writing. In case you are using this workbook on your own, without the support of a facilitator or a group, it is essential that you listen to your own emotional rhythm and write at your own pace. Take pauses when necessary and, ideally, use this workbook together with someone, be it a peer, a counselor, or a clinician. Check our suggestions on page 2-4.

DOI: 10.4324/9781003423270-4

3.1 Warming-up practices

3.1.1 Meditative writing

Estimated time: 5 minutes

> ## Guidelines for Group Practice
>
> If you are using this workbook as part of a writing group in an online setting, you can turn off your camera while you write, if you feel it will help you to be more present in your reflections. The facilitator will let you know when is a minute left before returning to the whole group, and then you can turn your camera on again.

In case you want to listen to this meditation, follow this link to find a recording.

For the next few minutes, bring your awareness inward, step by step.

Notice first your surroundings and briefly write about them. Describe the physical place where you are right now, as you transition into writing practice. Are there any colors, shapes, or objects that call your attention? Do you notice any smell, sound, or texture?

_____

_____

_____

Now, when you are ready, bring your attention to your body as it sits wherever you are. What parts of your body are in contact with the chair/floor? How do you know that your body is in contact with the chair/floor? Are there any physical sensations you can notice, such as warmth, coolness, a tingling sensation, or even discomfort?

Write down what you notice.

_____

_____

_____

_____

Is there something you need to do to feel more comfortable as you sit here today?

_____

_____

_____

_____

Now, bring your attention inwards, and list the thoughts that pass through or spin around in your mind. Are there any worries, concerns, images, or memories that arise?

_____

_____

_____

_____

Notice if there are any emotions present for you right now. At times, it is easier to notice what we "don't feel" than to know what we feel! It is also okay if today you feel rather numb or quiet. Thus, write down any emotion that is dominant, absent, or name the numbness or quietness. For writing, all you need is to begin wherever you are.

_____

_____

_____

_____

Now, set one or two intentions for today's practice. Examples of such intentions are as follows:

General intentions when writing

- To be as present as possible during today's session
- To feel closer to my child as I write
- To tolerate uncomfortable emotions that can arise during the session
- To take care of myself, and write at my own pace today, even if this means to take a pause from writing
- To create something raw, honest, and or beautiful
- Fill in this space with another intention if you find a personal one that is not mentioned above

Specific intentions for the week's theme

- To be as little judgmental as possible, and as caring as possible when I look back to my life story
- To look at suffering in my life with respect and honor, as a possibility to turn personal tragedies into heroic journeys
- Of course, please write another intention if you find a personal one that is not mentioned above)

_____

_____

_____

_____

My intention for this week's practice is:

_____

_____

_____

_____

_____

3.1.2   Check-in

Estimated time: 4 minutes

Sometimes we think that we do not have a right to feel certain ways about loss, or about our struggles to go about everyday life activities, this course included. This check-in is an opportunity for you to have an honest dialogue with yourself, as well as an opportunity to allow yourself to feel whatever you are feeling with compassion and acceptance. We will do this check-in each week, so you can have an overview of what you notice and learn about your emotional world throughout the course.

Give yourself a chance to fill in the first words that arise in your stream of consciousness. There are no right or wrong ways to feel, so do not think too much over the answer, and let words come to you with as little judgment as possible.

Throughout this program of therapeutic writing, all feelings are welcome because being aware and turning toward those feelings with curiosity and compassion will guide you in finding the themes, scenes, and lines in your writings. We are expecting that, at times, it will be difficult to find a word that is accurate enough about the way you feel and therefore we have also made a table (Table 3.1) that can serve you as inspiration to fill in the blanks for this practice.

- I feel _____ and
  _____ about my grief today.
- I don't feel _____ and
  _____ about my grief today.
- Today I feel, _____ and
  _____ about the writing course.
- Today I DON'T feel, _____ and
  _____ about the writing course.

Table 3.1 Suggestions for emotions for the weekly check-in practice

Possible emotions				Other emotions not present in the list (please add)
Adaptable	Confused	Jealous	Peaceful	
Agitated	Critical	Joyful	Pensive	
Alienated	Content	Light	Pessimistic	
Afraid	Curious	Loving	Positive	
Angry	Distressed	Lonely	Relaxed	

(Continued)

Table 3.1 (Continued)

Possible emotions				Other emotions not present in the list (please add)
Annoyed	Disturbed	Mad	Relieved	
Anxious	Empty	Melancholic	Resistant	
Apathetic	Euphoric	Miserable	Sad	
Ashamed	Excited	Mixed up	Safe	
Brave	Frustrated	Motivated	Serene	
Bitter	Gloomy	Mortified	Skeptical	
Bored	Grateful	Moody	Strong	
Bittersweet	Guilty/ Remorseful	Nauseated	Uncertain	
Calm	Happy	Negative	Unhappy	
Caring	Hopeful	Nostalgic	Vibrant	
Cautious	Humiliated	Numb	Vulnerable	
Chaotic	Humbled	Optimistic	Worried	
Confident	Infuriated	Outside of myself	Weak	
Comfortable	Inspired	Overwhelmed	Wonderful	

Note: The list of emotions suggested in this table is inspired by the overview of emotional categories in English available at The Berkeley Well-being Institute (Davis, n.d.), the Multiple Affect Adjective Checklist (Gotlib & Meyer, 1986), our clinical experience, and other words that our participants have used to describe their experiences.

3.3 PRACTICE: Introducing the dialogical self

3.3.1 *Reading poems as inspiration*

Estimated time: 5 minutes

Read this poem by Rumi:

> This human being is a guest house.
> Every morning there is a new arrival.
> A joy, a grief, a despair, some momentary awareness comes, as an unexpected visitor.
>
> Welcome and entertain them all!
> Even if they're a crowd of sorrows, who violently sweeps your house empty of its furniture,
> still treat each guest honorably,
> they may be clearing you out for some new delight.
>
> The dark thought, the shame, the malice,
> meet them at the door laughing, and invite them in.
>
> Be grateful for whoever comes, because each has been sent as a guest from beyond.

"The Guest House", by Jalal al-Din Rumi, translation copyright © 2001 by Dina Al-Mahdy, reprinted with permission. Egypt. www.dinaalmahdy.com

3.3.2 *Time for reflection*

Estimated time: 5 minutes

What are your impressions about the poem?

Was there any stanza that caught your attention or triggered you? If so, Which one?

Some participants find the stanza "Be grateful for whoever comes/because each has been sent as a guide from beyond" as triggering. This usually opens a discussion around gratitude. Some have mentioned that this reminds them of things they have heard from healthcare professionals and family members or friends: that they should feel grateful. However, this often makes them feel under pressure, angry, or misunderstood. How do you feel about gratitude?

Guidelines for Group Practice

What did the poem tell you?

Estimated time: 10 minutes

Share, if you want to, your impressions about the poem. What does this poem mean for you? Is there a stanza that touches your heart and if so, which one?

Learning Theory Together

Estimated time: 10 minutes

Dialogical self theory

The Dialogical Self Theory is an approach in psychology created by Professor Emeritus Hubert Hermans in the Netherlands (Hermans, Kempen & Van Loon, 1992; Hermans, 2001), and further developed by his colleagues and students all over the world.

Simply put, as we introduced on page 13, when thinking of the dialogical mind, we can say that the mind works like a theater or film set. In this theater or film set of the mind, there are many different characters that interact to form our sense of identity, often referred to as 'I-positions'. For example, we are simultaneously a father/mother, a cousin, a daughter/son, a friend, a person who is passionate about a sport and or art, and so on. In addition, in our minds, we have inner versions of other people we have interacted with, such as a favorite (or disliked) school teacher, a healthcare professional, a family member, a colleague, or even a wisdom figure who personifies our core values.

At any given moment, some of these characters in the mind can be more dominant while some others can be more silent. Likewise, at times, instead of specific characters, there are specific emotional aspects of yourself that become more dominant than others – yourself as angry, needy, and humorous. Taking perspective and observing with curiosity and compassion, the contents of our mind can give room for creativity and meaning-making.

3.4 PRACTICE: The art of editing our own texts

3.4.1 Time to take perspective

Estimated time: 15 minutes.

Look at what you have written as a home practice, or choose another text that you have available. Read it once more and reflect upon the following questions:

Who wrote this story? Is this written by the mother/father in me, the lonely spouse, a part of you that is angry or lost, etc.?

_____

_____

_____

Which characters are present in this story? Is there more than one? Are they speaking in a chorus, or different or even conflicting ways?

_____

_____

_____

Which feelings are present in this story? You might infer more than one, blended or tangled together, or arising in a sequence.

_____

_____

_____

_____

_____

Are there any dominant emotions/characters in this story? If so, which ones?

_____

_____

_____

_____

_____

Which emotions/characters are silent or absent in this story? Are any parts systematically marginalized or neglected, in a sense denied a speaking role on the stage? How would be performance change if they were given a leading role?

_____

_____

_____

_____

_____

Guidelines for Group Practice

Giving and receiving feedback about your writings

🕐 Estimated time: 30–35 minutes

If you are using this workbook as part of a writing group, you will be working in dyads or groups of three. Choose one of the texts that you have written as part of your home practice or any other text you feel comfortable sharing with others. Then, read it out loud for the person(s) they are working with. If you feel vulnerable or triggered by reading out loud, you can ask another person to read it out loud as you listen to your own words. Take turns in the speaker or listener role until each has had a chance to perform both parts and set a timer to prompt them when to switch roles. The facilitator might also give reminders about time, to help you keep on track.

NOTE: You do *not* need to write down your answers to the following questions; it is enough to focus on the dialogue with others. You are free to share as little or as much as you find it comfortable.

- *For the person sharing:* What do you feel right now after you have read this text? (or after listening to your partner read your story?)

- *For the person listening:* Begin by briefly saying something along the lines of "thanks for sharing," and then follow up with something like:

  - I noticed you repeated the theme/word _____ in your text. Could you describe more in detail what makes this theme/word important for you?
  - I'd like to hear more about what the "character _____" that you mention in your story was feeling.
  - This image about _____ touched my heart.
  - When I heard you saying _____, I could feel so deeply the heaviness of your grief.
  - It caught my attention that you mentioned _____ [a place/object/person/weather] in your text [e.g., garden, trolley, nurse, cloudy day]. That sounded _____ [important/beautiful/ominous] to me. Could you give me a fuller description or image of that?

- *For the person sharing:* <u>Take notes</u> on the feedback you receive from others. Given that writing about grief is a tender and vulnerable experience, it is natural that we forget some details of the feedback we receive.

- Change roles and make sure that each of you has the same time to share.

_____

_____

_____

_____

_____

_____

Guidelines for One-to-one Facilitation

In the setting of one-to-one facilitation such as peer-support or counseling, you as a facilitator can read out loud one of the texts the mourner has written and provide feedback about it. Follow the same suggestions as in the group practice. In most cases, as the facilitator you will not read a text back but instead mainly focus on holding space for the writer's story or text and the feelings, emotions, thoughts, images, and or memories that arise when reading it. However, in some scenarios, peer-support facilitators have written stories of their own and might feel like sharing them with the bereaved person. Don't feel any pressure to do so, as it needs to feel spontaneous and natural, but it can add an interesting dimension to the exchange. If that would be of interest, you might discuss it with the mourner directly.

3.5   PRACTICE: The guests of your inner house

Back to the metaphor of the mind being a theater or film set, this practice is an opportunity to tune your attention inwards and be in contact with how your grief process is unfolding here and now. During life ruptures, such as in the loss of a child, some parts of us become silent (or forgotten). These can be parts of us that we do not find the energy or motivation to bring forward such as yourself-as-daughter, partner, friend, artist, or athletes, just to name a few. This exercise is an invitation to reanimate them and allow them to contribute their strong qualities as resources to accompany you in your grieving.

3.5.1   Introducing the guests of your inner house

Estimated time: 10–12 minutes

Write down some of your very best memories with the main guests of your inner house (i.e., the characters in the theater or film set of your mind). What sense of wisdom, values, or attributes can you bring forward from these memories about how to cope with life right now? For example, from the mountain climber in me I could pick the value of perseverance, or the philosopher in me could contribute a sense of perspective on life's tragedies. Note that some of these 'I-positions' or aspects of your identity might even be playful or hopeful, such as the child in you.

_____

_____

_____

_____

_____

_____

_____

_____

_____

_____

3.6   Check out journaling

Estimated time: 4 minutes

Now that you are finishing this chapter, use some minutes to answer the following questions, without thinking too much about what you are to write. Answer in a way that feels spontaneous and genuine for you.

What have I learned about grief today?

_____

_____

_____

_____

_____

What have I learned about writing today?

_____

_____

_____

_____

_____

What have I learned about myself today?

_____

_____

_____

_____

_____

3.7   Further practice

Estimated time: 10 minutes

Write down a list of three of the characters of your inner house that you would like to have more contact with right now.

_____

_____

_____

Pick one of them.

_____

What kind of daily practices or rituals could help you to make this part of yourself more active, and to take better care of yourself?

Set a concrete goal for yourself, such as the one in this example:

Character: She who is still young within me
Goal: to train more/dance more
Behavioral goal: to do a 15-minute dance workout once a week with a YouTube video.

Note: It is important to think of it as a behavioral goal, a concrete action, independent of the emotions or thoughts associated with it. Indeed, we can dance even if sadly, or march around our neighborhood angrily. If we wait until we feel "motivated" to take an action step, we might wait a long time. The cognitive-behavioral psychiatrist, David Burns (1980), is fond of saying that *"action comes before motivation,"* wisely recognizing that concrete behavioral activation is more likely to lead to motivation than *vice versa*. It is natural that you can be sad or unmotivated given what you are going through. Self-care does not have to do with feeling great as a precondition to taking constructive action, but about carrying out activities that can make grief more bearable or bring balance in daily life. Think about it as a long-term investment for yourself, instead of only favoring short-term relief measures.

_____

_____

_____

_____

_____

_____

_____

_____

_____

_____

_____

_____

_____

_____

Chapter 4

Anger, shame compassion, and self-compassion

Weekly theme(s): Psychoeducation and experiential learning about anger, shame, compassion, and self-compassion.

Estimated time: 2–2.5 hours, including two pauses of 10 minutes each.

Embracing compassion: One of the core emotions associated with grief is sadness. This makes it, often, easier for yourself or others to show sympathy, empathy, and or compassion toward sadness, than toward other emotions. In contrast, many of the persons we have worked with feel, therefore, alone in coping with difficult emotions such as anger, guilt, and shame. As you write this week, give yourself an opportunity to learn from the wisdom that these other difficult emotions behold.

Gentle reminder: We calculated the timeframes and the intensity that we indicate for each assignment based on our experiences facilitating online groups of therapeutic writing. In case you are using this workbook on your own, without the support of a facilitator or a group, it is essential that you listen to your own emotional rhythm and write at your own pace. Take pauses when necessary and, ideally, use this workbook together with someone, be it a peer, a counselor, or a clinician. Check our suggestions on page 2-4.

DOI: 10.4324/9781003423270-5

4.1 Warm-up

4.1.1 Meditative writing

🕒 Estimated time: 5 minutes

> **Guidelines for Group Practice**
>
> If you are using this workbook as part of a writing group in an online setting, you can turn off your camera while you write, if you feel it will help you to be more present in your reflections. The facilitator will let you know when is a minute left before returning to the whole group, and then you can turn your camera on again.

🔊 In case you want to listen to this meditation, follow this link to find a recording.

For the next few minutes, bring your awareness inward, step by step.

Notice first your surroundings and briefly write about them. Describe the physical place where you are right now, as you transition into writing practice. Are there any colors, shapes, or objects that call your attention? Do you notice any smell, sound, or texture?

_____

_____

_____

Now, when you are ready, bring your attention to your body as it sits wherever you are. What parts of your body are in contact with the chair/floor? How do you know that your body is in contact with the chair/floor? Are there any physical sensations you can notice, such as warmth, coolness, a tingling sensation, or even discomfort?

Write down what you notice.

_____

_____

_____

_____

Is there something you need to do to feel more comfortable as you sit here today?

_____

_____

_____

Now, bring your attention inwards, and list the thoughts that pass through or spin around in your mind. Are there any worries, concerns, images, or memories that arise?

_____

_____

_____

_____

Notice if there are any emotions present for you right now. At times, it is easier to notice what we "don't feel" than to know what we feel! It is also okay if today you feel rather numb or quiet. Thus, write down any emotion that is dominant, absent, or name the numbness or quietness. For writing, all you need is to begin wherever you are.

_____

_____

_____

_____

Now, set one or two intentions for today's practice. Examples of such intentions are as follows:

General intentions when writing

- To be as present as possible during today's session
- To feel closer to my child as I write
- To tolerate uncomfortable emotions that can arise during the session
- To take care of myself, and write at my own pace today, even if this means to take a pause from writing.
- To create something raw, honest, and or beautiful
- Fill in this space with another intention if you find a personal one that is not mentioned above.

Specific intentions for the week's theme

- To be curious about the ways in which anger, guilt, and or shame show up today, instead of judging it or avoiding uncomfortable feelings as much.
- To trust that anger, guilt and shame are a natural part of grieving and that focusing on them explicitly will be helpful for my process.

_____

_____

_____

_____

My intention for this week's practice is:

_____

_____

_____

_____

_____

4.1.2 Check-in

Estimated time: 4 minutes

Sometimes we think that we do not have a right to feel certain ways about loss, or about our struggles to go about everyday life activities, this course included. This check-in is an opportunity for you to have an honest dialogue with yourself, as well as an opportunity to allow yourself to feel whatever you are feeling with compassion and acceptance. We will do this check-in each week, so you can have an overview of what you notice and learn about your emotional world throughout the course.

Give yourself a chance to fill in the first words that arise in your stream of consciousness. There are no right or wrong ways to feel, so do not think too much over the answer, and let words come to you with as little judgment as possible.

Throughout this program of therapeutic writing, all feelings are welcome because being aware and turning toward those feelings with curiosity and compassion will guide you in finding the themes, scenes, and lines in your writings. We are expecting that, at times, it will be difficult to find a word that is accurate enough about the way you feel and therefore we have also made a table (Table 4.1) that can serve you as inspiration to fill in the blanks for this practice.

- I feel _____ and _____ about my grief today.
- I don't feel _____ and _____ about my grief today.
- Today I feel, _____ and _____ about the writing course.
- Today I DON'T feel, _____ and _____ about the writing course.

Table 4.1 Suggestions for emotions for the weekly check-in practice

Possible emotions				Other emotions not present in the list (please add)
Adaptable	Confused	Jealous	Peaceful	
Agitated	Critical	Joyful	Pensive	
Alienated	Content	Light	Pessimistic	
Afraid	Curious	Loving	Positive	
Angry	Distressed	Lonely	Relaxed	

(Continued)

Table 4.1 (Continued)

Possible emotions				Other emotions not present in the list (please add)
Annoyed	Disturbed	Mad	Relieved	
Anxious	Empty	Melancholic	Resistant	
Apathetic	Euphoric	Miserable	Sad	
Ashamed	Excited	Mixed up	Safe	
Brave	Frustrated	Motivated	Serene	
Bitter	Gloomy	Mortified	Skeptical	
Bored	Grateful	Moody	Strong	
Bittersweet	Guilty/ Remorseful	Nauseated	Uncertain	
Calm	Happy	Negative	Unhappy	
Caring	Hopeful	Nostalgic	Vibrant	
Cautious	Humiliated	Numb	Vulnerable	
Chaotic	Humbled	Optimistic	Worried	
Confident	Infuriated	Outside of myself	Weak	
Comfortable	Inspired	Overwhelmed	Wonderful	

Note: The list of emotions suggested in this table is inspired by the overview of emotional categories in English available at The Berkeley Well-being Institute (Davis, n.d.), the Multiple Affect Adjective Checklist (Gotlib &Meyer, 1986), our clinical experience, and other words that our participants have used to describe their experiences.

Learning Theory Together

Estimated time: 10 minutes

On compassion and self-compassion toward anger and shame

Images such as a lighthouse, a torch, or a candle, can be used as symbols of honor, inner strength, or love. These symbols, often incorporated in artistic expressions, can help us lean into the beauty beneath the tragic nature of life. Please do not confuse these metaphors with the idea that you must "look at the bright side" of life. When one has experienced something as terrible as the death of a child, it can be also important to accept the darkness. One of the participants in the writing courses we have conducted put it this way: *As a bereaved person you might have a strong need to share the rawness of your grief without censorship.*

The arts, either in words or in images or forms, can help us portray difficult emotions and help us explore their function and significance. Contemplating a work of art, even if it is a piece that expresses suffering, can help us feel seen and understood: it can confirm that we are not alone in our suffering, that it is human. In the case of grief, there are many different examples we can draw on for inspiration. For instance, the Mexican artist Frida Kahlo graphically depicted her experience of going through abortion, as well as various sides of her identity and dynamics in her relationships, in revealing self-portraits. In quite a different form the *Sonatorrek*, one of the greatest Viking sagas, poetically and powerfully gave voice to the grief of a man who lost his son.

The more we can dive into the experiences and expressions of grief, whatever form that might take, the more we can feel, tolerate, and meet with understanding and compassion. But what is compassion after all? When we acknowledge someone's suffering, understand the challenges they are going through, feel for them, and are motivated to alleviate or reduce such suffering, then we are being compassionate (Shulz & Monin, 2018; Lehmann, 2018). By extension, *self*-compassion involves investigating our own suffering with understanding, friendship, patience, and empowerment (Neff, 2016).

When considering what the experience of losing a child can entail, one of the most compassionate expressions we have found is to recognize that *this is unfair!* This can be a form of validation of the profound sense of violation that this tragedy happened to your child, to your family, and to you. The death of a child can lead to strong experiences of anger, guilt, and shame that shatter our understanding of ourselves, who we are, and who we can become in the wake of a traumatic loss. Let's explore in detail each of these emotions to learn to use them as a source of meaning and direction.

Important functions of emotions

According to traditions such as Emotion-focused Therapy (EFT), our emotions can be *primary* or *secondary* (Greenberg, 2006). When our emotions are primary, they relate to our raw responses to specific situations in the present moment. When our emotions are secondary, they cover up other feelings, hiding the core vulnerability underneath, which we have not yet been ready to contact, acknowledge, or work with.

Anger, as a *primary* emotion, is signaling that what we care about is threatened, has been attacked or destroyed. It is a natural reaction to injustice (Pascual Leone & Paivio, 2013). As a *secondary* emotion, anger can cover up or defend us from more vulnerable feelings such as sadness, shame, or fear (Pascual Leone & Paivio, 2013).

According to our experience with many bereaved mothers and fathers, one of the strongest triggers for anger in relation to grief is that it challenges parents' sense of identity. This was especially so for many women. The death of a child appears for many people to violate the very premise of parenthood, and raises many questions such as *Can I still be considered a mother/father?*, or *Why did this happen to me, or to my child?*

The following practice might give you some insight and tools to work with in dealing with anger and grief:

4.2   PRACTICE: In contact with anger

4.2.1   *Fill in the blanks...*

Estimated time: 8 minutes

It feels unfair that…

_____

_____

Right now, I feel anger about… (e.g., life, a partner, a medical procedure going wrong…)

_____

_____

What anger has taught me/What I can learn about anger is…
   Note: Ask yourself the proprioceptive question, What do I mean by "X"? By "X" I mean…
(See page 17)

_____

_____

4.2.2   *What did you notice?*

🕒 Estimated time: 3 minutes

What did you notice when writing during this practice?

_____

_____

_____

_____

Guidelines for Group Practice

🕒 Estimated time: 12 minutes.

If you are using this workbook as part of a writing group, you will have an opportunity to share with one another what you noticed while undergoing this practice. You do not need to write down the answer, unless you want to do so. This group practice is mainly about sharing in the form of an oral dialogue with one another.

   Either in a dyad or in groups of three, assign turns for who will start being the listener, and who will start sharing. If necessary, plan also who would have the next turn sharing. Assign someone the responsibility for setting an alarm to track time and ensure that each person in the group has an even time to share. The facilitator might give reminders about time, to help you stay on track.

For the person listening:

- Place your hand on your heart, may you feel it helps you to feel grounded as you listen to one another.
- If someone cries, for instance, remind them that it is ok to cry and hold space for their tears. The aim of this group is to hold space for our feelings, without necessarily urging to fix them or lessen them.
- Avoid the urge to jump into the conversation with your own story. You might find similarities between what your peer is sharing. You might also feel the urge to give some advice that has helped you personally. However, in this practice, we prioritize crafting a space of safety for our emotions no matter what they are, and the trust that our classmates will find their way. That is, this practice is about giving

space to the other person to be in contact with themselves. Since they are the experts in their own grief, we need to trust that they will find resources that work for them.
- Once the person is done reading their writings:
  - Thank them for their courage.
  - Ask: how do you feel now, after having read this text to us?

- Change turns and make sure that each of you has the same time.

4.3   PRACTICE: How would you treat a fellow bereaved parent?

4.3.1   *Writing a compassionate letter to a fellow bereaved parent*

Estimated time: 15 minutes

This practice is inspired from a self-compassion practice originally introduced by Kristin Neff and Chris Germer (2018) where people are invited to write a letter to an imaginary friend about a difficult experience.

In our case, we address explicitly the theme of grief, and we ask you to write a letter for a fellow bereaved parent. As you write the letter, have these questions in mind:

- What would you tell them about the process of grief?
- How would you encourage them to be kind and compassionate with themselves? Avoid unsolicited advice.
- Without aiming at fixing their feelings, what would you tell them to comfort them in the darkness of their grief?
- Write with a warm and caring style, similar to the way in which you would have typically spoken to a nother peer who is going through a difficult period with their grief.

Guidelines for Group Practice

If you are using this workbook as part of a writing group, you will write this letter directly to the classmate with whom you were doing the previous practice, and they would, in exchange, write a letter back to you. Mind that you will actually read or have the other person read the letter afterward!

_____

_____

_____

_____

_____

_____

_____

_____

_____

_____

_____

_____

_____

_____

_____

_____

_____

_____

_____

_____

_____

_____

_____

4.3.2   *What do you notice?*

Estimated time: 5 minutes

What do you notice after having written this letter?

_____

_____

_____

How similar or different is this letter compared to the one you would want to receive from a caring friend?

_____

_____

_____

Guidelines for Group Practice

🕐 Estimated time: 15 minutes.

In the same dyads as earlier, read the letter to the person you wrote it to, or have them read it themselves. While listening to one another, follow these guidelines:

- Place your hand on your heart as you listen, if you feel it helps you to keep yourself grounded.
- If someone is crying, then remind them that it is ok to cry, and allow some silent space for these tears without rushing into fixing something.
- Avoid the urge to interrupt one another to share parts of your own story or give advice. While it is natural that you will make some associations as you listen, this is a practice of holding space and trusting the other person will find their way with their own resources.
- All emotions are welcome. We need a safe space for our emotional experiences.
- Thank one another after a round of sharing ends, before moving to the next person.
- Monitor time and respect the time division. Perhaps set an alarm on one of your phones so that you can relax into the listening while keeping track of the practice.

After each person has finished reading, and before moving to the next person, ask these questions:

For the reader: What do you feel right now after reading this piece?
For the listener: What do you feel right now after listening to this letter?

- Remember to thank each other for sharing, briefly say "Thanks for sharing" or something along these lines.
- You can also briefly validate their experiences, saying, for example, "I understand why you would feel…"

4.3.3   Time to take perspective: How do I usually talk to myself about grief?

🕐 Estimated time: 10 minutes

Some of the following questions are modified by the follow-up exercise from Kristin Neff and Chris Germer (2018), and the "loss characterization" technique where one is invited to write about grief using a friendly tone toward oneself (Neimeyer, 2006). We have also added some questions on our own. Take some minutes to reflect upon the ways in which you usually talk to yourself about grief:

• What do you usually do when you are feeling emotionally triggered by grief?

_____

_____

_____

• What are the typical thoughts that arise when you are triggered?

_____

_____

_____

• What would you say to yourself when struggling the most with grief?

_____

_____

_____

• How similar or different are the tone and the words you used in the letter to a fellow bereaved parent, and the words you tend to use when speaking to yourself?

_____

_____

_____

• If there was a big difference between the tone in the letter to a fellow bereaved parent and the tone of your inner voice when you are struggling with your own grief, why do you think this is the case?

_____

_____

_____

_____

_____

_____

_____

Now that you have gained some insight into the potential differences between writing a letter to another bereaved parent and the way in which you speak to yourself about grief, set the intention of having more dialogues with yourself in a gentle, caring, and patient manner.

- What would happen if you would treat yourself with more kindness and compassion as you cope with your grief?

_____

_____

_____

4.5   Check out journaling

Estimated time: 4 minutes

Now that you are finishing this chapter, use some minutes to answer the following questions, without thinking too much about what you are to write. Answer in a way that feels spontaneous and genuine for you.

What have I learned about grief today?

_____

_____

_____

What have I learned about writing today?

_____

_____

_____

What have I learned about myself today?

_____

_____

_____

4.6 Further practice

🕐 Estimated time: 8 minutes

What act of compassion could you carry out this week to better take care of your suffering? Try to translate general goals into specific behavioral goals or actions that you actually can do, as in the following examples.

- *Example of general goal:* to talk to myself in a more friendly tone

  Behavioral goal: to write down three post-it notes that I can hang in different places when I catch myself being self-critical, and which remind me to have more compassion for myself in this circumstance.

- *Example of a general goal:* to have a grieving ritual

  Behavioral goal: light a candle and spend some minutes honoring my child. Make a grief drawer at home that includes precious reminders of the child – perhaps an ultrasound image, a photograph, a receiving blanket, or a plush toy you purchased as the child's first gift. Then spend 15–30 minutes bringing out those objects and writing about them, before replacing them in the drawer for a future visit.

  My behavioral goal(s) for this week:

  _____

  _____

  _____

Chapter 5

Loving-kindness as we tend to our life story

Weekly theme(s): Psychoeducation and experiential learning practices around the inherent relationship between love and grief. How grief shapes life vs. How life shapes grief.

Estimated time: 2–2.5 hours, including two pauses of 10 minutes each.

Embracing compassion: Grief affects the way we live, and the way we have lived affects the way we grieve. This week we will investigate different dimensions of your life story. We are aware that during your life you are likely to have had other experiences that have been difficult for you, even if few compare with the loss of your child. We are also aware that right now, life might feel messy and that some areas have been unattended and unbalanced as you contend with your grief. There is, of course, also wisdom underneath the suffering that you have had to embrace, even if it takes some searching to find it.

Gentle reminder: We calculated the timeframes and the intensity that we indicate for each assignment based on our experiences facilitating online groups of therapeutic writing. In case you are using this workbook on your own, without the support of a facilitator or a group, it is essential that you listen to your own emotional rhythm and write at your own pace. Take pauses when necessary and, ideally, use this workbook together with someone, be it a peer, a counselor, or a clinician. Check our suggestions on page 2-4.

DOI: 10.4324/9781003423270-6

5.1 Warm-up

5.1.1   Meditative writing

Estimated time: 5 minutes

Guidelines for Group Practice

If you are using this workbook as part of a writing group in an online setting, you can turn off your camera while you write, if you feel it will help you to be more present in your reflections. The facilitator will let you know when is a minute left before returning to the whole group, and then you can turn your camera on again.

In case you want to listen to this meditation, follow this link to find a recording.

For the next few minutes, bring your awareness inward, step by step.

Notice first your surroundings and briefly write about them. Describe the physical place where you are right now, as you transition into writing practice. Are there any colors, shapes, or objects that call your attention? Do you notice any smell, sound, or texture?

_____

_____

_____

Now, when you are ready, bring your attention to your body as it sits wherever you are. What parts of your body are in contact with the chair? How do you know that your body is in contact with the chair? Are there any physical sensations you can notice, such as warmth, coolness, a tingling sensation, or even pain?

Write down what you notice.

_____

_____

_____

_____

Is there something you need to do to feel more comfortable as you sit?

_____

_____

_____

_____

Now, bring your attention inwards, and list the thoughts that pass through or spin around in your mind. Are there any worries, concerns, images, or memories that arise?

Notice if there are any emotions present for you right now. At times, it is easier to notice what we "don't feel" than to know what we feel! It is also okay if today you feel rather numb or quiet. Thus, write down any emotion that is dominant, absent, or name the numbness or quietness. For writing, all you need is to begin wherever you are.

Now, set one or two intentions for today's practice. Examples of such intentions are:

General intentions when writing

- To be as present as possible during today's session
- To feel closer to my child as I write
- To tolerate uncomfortable emotions that can arise during the session
- To take care of myself, and write at my own pace today, even if this means to take a pause from writing.
- To create something raw, honest, and or beautiful
- Fill in this space with another intention if you find a personal one that is not mentioned above.

Specific intentions to the week's theme

- To be curious about the different shapes that love has in my personal life, even if some of these are unexpected.
- To trust that it is possible to treat myself with loving-kindness in the midst of the chaotic feelings of grief.

My intention for this week's practice is:

5.1.2   *Check-in*

🕐 Estimated time: 4 minutes

Sometimes we think that we do not have a right to feel certain ways about loss, or about our struggles to go about everyday life activities, this course included. This check-in is an opportunity for you to have an honest dialogue with yourself, as well as an opportunity to allow yourself to feel whatever you are feeling with compassion and acceptance. We will do this check-in each week, so you can have an overview of what you notice and learn about your emotional world throughout the course.

Give yourself a chance to fill in the first words that arise in your stream of consciousness. There are no right or wrong ways to feel, so do not think too much over the answer, and let words come to you with as little judgment as possible.

Throughout this program of therapeutic writing, all feelings are welcome because being aware and turning toward those feelings with curiosity and compassion will guide you in finding the themes, scenes, and lines in your writings. We are expecting that, at times, it will be difficult to find a word that is accurate enough about the way you feel and therefore we have also made a table (Table 5.1) that can serve you as inspiration to fill in the blanks for this practice.

- I feel _____ and
_____ about my grief today.
- I don't feel _____ and
_____ about my grief today.
- Today I feel, _____ and
_____ about the writing course.
- Today I DON'T feel, _____ and
_____ about the writing course.

Table 5.1 Suggestions for emotions for the weekly check-in practice

Possible emotions				Other emotions not present in the list (please add)
Adaptable	Confused	Jealous	Peaceful	
Agitated	Critical	Joyful	Pensive	
Alienated	Content	Light	Pessimistic	
Afraid	Curious	Loving	Positive	
Angry	Distressed	Lonely	Relaxed	
Annoyed	Disturbed	Mad	Relieved	
Anxious	Empty	Melancholic	Resistant	
Apathetic	Euphoric	Miserable	Sad	
Ashamed	Excited	Mixed up	Safe	
Brave	Frustrated	Motivated	Serene	
Bitter	Gloomy	Mortified	Skeptical	
Bored	Grateful	Moody	Strong	
Bittersweet	Guilty/ Remorseful	Nauseated	Uncertain	
Calm	Happy	Negative	Unhappy	

Table 5.1 (Continued)

Possible emotions				Other emotions not present in the list (please add)
Caring	Hopeful	Nostalgic	Vibrant	
Cautious	Humiliated	Numb	Vulnerable	
Chaotic	Humbled	Optimistic	Worried	
Confident	Infuriated	Outside of myself	Weak	
Comfortable	Inspired	Overwhelmed	Wonderful	

Note: The list of emotions suggested in this table is inspired by the overview of emotional categories in English available at The Berkeley Well-being Institute (Davis, n.d.), the Multiple Affect Adjective Checklist (Gotlib & Meyer, 1986), our clinical experience, and other words that our participants have used to describe their experiences.

5.2 PRACTICE: Loving-kindness maps

Being surrounded by loving-kindness and being able to provide it to others is one of the greatest aspirations for us human beings and one of the values that imbues our lives with meaning. When love is threatened or absent in one or another dimension of life, then that conflict or absence can become a source of despair and meaninglessness. During this practice, we will encourage you to investigate different dimensions of your personal life, to gain an understanding of the ways in which you feel love and or long for love in each of these dimensions.

5.2.1 Answer to the following questions

Estimated time: 5 minutes

What words of wisdom have motivated you when you have been through difficult life challenges? For example, a book, a poem, or a song may have inspired you in other challenging moments of your life story. Inspiration can also arise in a conversation you have had with someone. Write any phrases that hold meaning for you in the space below, or summarize the gist of this life philosophy or outlook.

_____

_____

_____

_____

Which of your personal qualities can you lean on when you are facing challenges in life?

_____

_____

_____

_____

5.2.2   *Mapping loving-kindness in my life*

🕐 Estimated time: 10 minutes

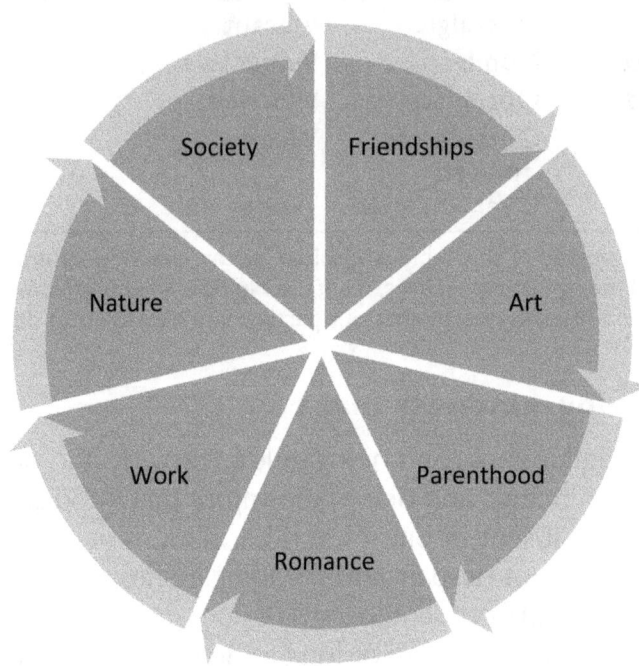

Answer to the following questions:

- In which of the contexts of this figure do you currently experience giving and or receiving loving-kindness as challenging?

_____

_____

_____

_____

_____

- In what ways is this challenging for you?

_____

_____

_____

_____

_____

- In which of the contexts of the figure could you give yourself more loving-kindness?

_____

_____

_____

_____

_____

- In what unexpected ways have you received love/care while dealing with your grief?

_____

_____

_____

_____

_____

Guidelines for Group Practice

Listening with our hearts

🕐 Estimated time: 15 minutes

If you are using this workbook as part of a writing group, you will work in a dyad or in a group of three. Assign turns for who will start being the listener, and who will start sharing. Assign someone the responsibility for setting an alarm to track time and ensure that each person in the group has an even time to share. The group facilitator might as well give reminders about time, so as to help you stay on track.
   Take turns answering the following questions:

What did you notice about yourself and your life story as you answered the previous questions?
How is this, possibly, giving you other perspectives about grief?

   While listening to one another, follow these guidelines:

For the person listening:

- Place your hand on your heart, may you feel it helps you to feel grounded as you listen to one another.

- If someone cries, for instance, remind them that it is ok to cry and hold space for their tears. The aim of this group is to hold space for our feelings, without necessarily urging to fix them or lessen them
- Avoid the urge to jump into the conversation with your own story. You might find similarities between what your peer is sharing. You might also feel the urge to give some advice that has helped you personally. However, in this practice, we prioritize crafting a space of safety for our emotions no matter what they are, and the trust that our classmates will find their way. That is, this practice is about giving space to the other person to be in contact with themselves. Since they are the experts in their own grief, we need to trust that they will find resources that work for them.
- Once the person is done reading their writings:
  - Ask: What do you feel right now after reading this piece?
  - Then, briefly say "Thanks for sharing".

- Change turns and make sure that each of you has the same time to share.

Learning theory together

On love and time

When people say things along the lines of "you shouldn't be so sad because the baby was not alive for so long," or "luckily the child died so soon; it would have been harder if they were older when they died," even with the best of intentions, these comments can hurt, and make parents feel misunderstood and their grief underestimated or dismissed as invalid.

Love cannot be measured in terms of chronological time. Love is qualitative, not quantitative. If love were to have a measure, it would be the intensity of your feelings, the future you imagined as a parent, your wishes for your child, as well as all the different practical plans and arrangements you have worked to put in place during the pregnancy, birth, and tragically, the funeral.

Some of the participants in the research groups that led to the development of this workbook (Lehmann et al., 2022; Lehmann et al., 2023) have expressed that this is an ambiguous kind of grief, leaving them with doubts about the nature of their identity as parents, as well as with challenges in understanding the impact that grief has had on their perception of time. Some parents have even wondered whether or not there should be a space for suffering in their lives. For instance, some who have lost an only child have asked questions such as "Am I still considered a parent?" or, "Do I have a right to grieve for so long?"

Grief disrupts the flow of our lives. We grieve both what has happened to us, and that which we had imagined but that never occurred, as the loss of dreams can wound us as much as the loss of a cherished past or present. We have found this anonymous poem to convey the power of storytelling in honoring our loved ones and perhaps making sense of grief:

"Do you have a magic spell to return someone to life?" she asked.
"No," the witch said, "I am sorry".

"Oh."

"Why don't you tell me about them?"

"Will that bring them back?"

"For us. For a little while. Stories are a different kind of magic."
Anonymous (If any of the readers of this workbook identify
the author, please contact www.lub.no to let us know).

This anonymous poem also reminds us that writing can take the form of dialogue with other parts of ourselves, the people we are grieving, the healthcare system, a partner, a spiritual entity or imaginary entity, and more.

In addition, when revising your life story in the light of love, you might become aware that grief affects the way you live, as much as the way you have lived affects the way you grieve. As vulnerable as this acknowledgment can be, it is crucial to bring compassion and self-care toward those tender spots in your life story, bringing understanding to them. Remember, within the framework of therapeutic writing, you are the editor of your life story: you might not be able to change the tragic experiences that have occurred to you throughout life, but you might be able to narrate these stories with compassion, forgiveness, hope, bravery, or any other value that feels genuine. All in all, this is a process, and you are not alone in it, even if it can feel so at times. That is also why we want to encourage you to look for support might you feel vulnerable. Whether you reach out to a family member, a friend, a help hotline, a therapist, a peer, a mentor, or a spiritual guide, trust that support is available when you need it.

5.3 PRACTICE: Narrating Your Grief Story

5.3.1 *Telling your grief story*

🕐 Estimated time: 20 minutes

Even when we want to, it is hard to find words to express the intensity of grief and the ways in which it affects our lives. A trick that can help us when writing about difficult experiences is to write from a third-person perspective as if someone else were writing your story. That is, if you are a bereaved parent instead of writing *"I feel…"*, you might write *"He/She/They feel…"*. In this practice, you are writing about what grief is like in your own life, and who you are in light of it. Think about novels you might have read or films you might have watched in which the narrator seems to know everything, although we do not know exactly who this speaker or writer is. This invisible narrator will be telling the story of your own grief. Think of this voice as a kind, friendly, forgiving voice who intends to tell your story with respect and honor.

Lorraine Hedtke (2012) suggests something like this when she encourages us to share appreciative memories or comments of the deceased in "introducing a loved one," and Robert Neimeyer (2006) suggests that an even more personal exercise can be writing a "loss characterization" of oneself from a similar compassionate perspective. Here we suggest that you do so in a free-form way, giving attention to what is importance to you. Afterward, we will provide you with some follow-up questions that can help you sift through and process the description of your grieving self that results. Of course, feel free to change the pronouns to make them match your gender.

Loss Characterization

In the space that follows, please write a character sketch of _____ [your name], in light of their loss. Write it just as if she were the principal character in a book, movie, or play. Write it as it might be written by a friend who knew her very intimately and very sympathetically, perhaps better than anyone really could know her. Be sure to write it in the third person. For example, start out by saying, _____ is…

_____

_____

_____

_____

_____

_____

_____

_____

_____

Processing your Character Sketch

1 Briefly state, what the world looks like through this character's eyes. What kind of place is it, and what is the role of other people?

_____

_____

_____

_____

_____

2 Are there any specific descriptions for this character's personality or values? What kind of future is this character moving toward?

_____

_____

_____

_____

_____

3 Are there certain themes or emotions that come up again and again in this sketch? Are these despairing or hopeful? What do they suggest about the issues the character is wrestling with?

_____

_____

_____

_____

_____

4 Is the character's basic meaning in life challenged, affirmed, or clarified by the loss? Who might support the character in making sense of this experience?

_____

_____

_____

_____

_____

5 What seems to be shaping this character's destiny? How much control does the character have in life, and how much does this matter?

_____

_____

_____

_____

_____

- What do you as an intimate friend hope that grief is teaching this character about life? How would you advise the character to tackle the challenges ahead?

_____

_____

_____

_____

- If this character were to strengthen the bond with the child further in the coming years, what form might this take?

_____

_____

_____

_____

5.3.2   What did you notice?

🕐 Estimated time: 3 minutes

What did you notice when writing during this practice?

_____

_____

_____

_____

_____

Guidelines for Group Practice

🕐 Estimated time: 15 minutes

If you are using this workbook as part of a writing group, you will have an opportunity to share with one another what you noticed while undergoing this practice.

5.4   Check out journaling

🕐 Estimated time: 4 minutes

Now that you are finishing this chapter, use some minutes to answer the following questions, without thinking too much about what you are to write. Answer in a way that feels spontaneous and genuine for you.

What have I learned about grief today?

_____

_____

_____

What have I learned about writing today?

_____

_____

_____

What have I learned about myself today?

_____

_____

_____

5.5   Further practice

Estimated time: 10 minutes

Keep writing the "He/She/They who grieve." Include these prompts in your writing: "hands," "the old windows," "to light a candle." What emotions (if any) appear in this story? If this text were to give hope to its reader, how could a sense of loneliness be transformed along the storytelling?

Chapter 6

From self-blame to life lessons

Weekly theme(s): Psychoeducation and experiential learning practices about personal values, meaning.

Estimated length of the session: 2–2.5 hours, including two pauses of 10 minutes each.

Embracing compassion: When in contact with difficult emotions such as sadness, jealousy, anger, guilt, or shame, many of us can blame ourselves for what has happened in our lives. Considering values that are relevant to our life story can help us to take perspective from inner criticism and embrace compassion.

Gentle reminder: We calculated the timeframes and the intensity that we indicate for each assignment based on our experiences facilitating online groups of therapeutic writing. In case you are using this workbook on your own, without the support of a facilitator or a group, it is essential that you listen to your own emotional rhythm and write at your own pace. Take pauses when necessary and, ideally, use this workbook together with someone, be it a peer, a counselor, or a clinician. Check our suggestions on page 2-4.

DOI: 10.4324/9781003423270-7

6.1 Warm-up

6.1.1 Meditative writing

🕐 Estimated time: 5 minutes

> **Guidelines for Group Practice**
>
> If you are using this workbook as part of a writing group in an online setting, you can turn off your camera while you write, if you feel it will help you to be more present in your reflections. The facilitator will let you know when is a minute left before returning to the whole group, and then you can turn your camera on again.

🔊 In case you want to listen to this meditation, follow this link to find a recording.

For the next few minutes, bring your awareness inward, step by step.

Notice first your surroundings and briefly write about them. Describe the physical place where you are right now, as you transition into writing practice. Are there any colors, shapes, or objects that call your attention? Do you notice any smell, sound, or texture?

_____

_____

_____

Now, when you are ready, bring your attention to your body as it sits wherever you are. What parts of your body are in contact with the chair? How do you know that your body is in contact with the chair? Are there any physical sensations you can notice, such as warmth, coolness, a tingling sensation, or even pain?

Write down what you notice.

_____

_____

_____

_____

Is there something you need to do to feel more comfortable as you sit?

_____

_____

_____

_____

Now, bring your attention inwards, and list the thoughts that pass through or spin around in your mind. Are there any worries, concerns, images, or memories that arise?

_____

_____

_____

_____

Notice if there are any emotions present for you right now. At times, it is easier to notice what we "don't feel" than to know what we feel! It is also okay if today you feel rather numb or quiet. Thus, write down any emotion that is dominant, absent, or name the numbness or quietness. For writing, all you need is to begin wherever you are.

_____

_____

_____

_____

Now, set one or two intentions for today's practice. Examples of such intentions are as follows:

General intentions when writing

- To be as present as possible during today's session
- To feel closer to my child as I write.
- To tolerate uncomfortable emotions that can arise during the session
- To take care of myself, and write at my own pace today, even if this means to take a pause from writing.
- To create something raw, honest, and or beautiful.
- Fill in this space with another intention if you find a personal one that is not mentioned above.

Specific intentions for the week's theme

- To be curious about the different shapes that love has in my personal life, even if some of these are unexpected.
- To trust that it is possible to treat myself with loving-kindness in the midst of the chaotic feelings of grief.

My intention for this week's practice is:

_____

_____

_____

6.1.2 Check-in

🕐 Estimated time: 4 minutes

Sometimes we think that we do not have a right to feel certain ways about loss, or about our struggles to go about everyday life activities, this course included. This check-in is an opportunity for you to have an honest dialogue with yourself, as well as an opportunity to allow yourself to feel whatever you are feeling with compassion and acceptance. We will do this check-in each week, so you can have an overview of what you notice and learn about your emotional world throughout the course.

Give yourself a chance to fill in the first words that arise in your stream of consciousness. There are no right or wrong ways to feel, so do not think too much over the answer, and let words come to you with as little judgment as possible.

Throughout this program of therapeutic writing, all feelings are welcome because being aware and turning toward those feelings with curiosity and compassion will guide you in finding the themes, scenes, and lines in your writings. We are expecting that, at times, it will be difficult to find a word that is accurate enough about the way you feel and therefore we have also made a table (Table 6.1) that can serve you as inspiration to fill in the blanks for this practice.

- I feel _____ and
  _____ about my grief today.
- I don't feel _____ and
  _____ about my grief today.
- Today I feel, _____ and
  _____ about the writing course.
- Today I DON'T feel, _____ and
  _____ about the writing course.

Table 6.1 Suggestions for emotions for the weekly check-in practice

Possible emotions				Other emotions not present in the list (please add)
Adaptable	Confused	Jealous	Peaceful	
Agitated	Critical	Joyful	Pensive	
Alienated	Content	Light	Pessimistic	
Afraid	Curious	Loving	Positive	
Angry	Distressed	Lonely	Relaxed	
Annoyed	Disturbed	Mad	Relieved	
Anxious	Empty	Melancholic	Resistant	
Apathetic	Euphoric	Miserable	Sad	
Ashamed	Excited	Mixed up	Safe	
Brave	Frustrated	Motivated	Serene	
Bitter	Gloomy	Mortified	Skeptical	
Bored	Grateful	Moody	Strong	
Bittersweet	Guilty/ Remorseful	Nauseated	Uncertain	
Calm	Happy	Negative	Unhappy	

(Continued)

Table 6.1 (Continued)

Possible emotions				Other emotions not present in the list (please add)
Caring	Hopeful	Nostalgic	Vibrant	
Cautious	Humiliated	Numb	Vulnerable	
Chaotic	Humbled	Optimistic	Worried	
Confident	Infuriated	Outside of myself	Weak	
Comfortable	Inspired	Overwhelmed	Wonderful	

Note: The list of emotions suggested in this table is inspired by the overview of emotional categories in English available at The Berkeley Well-being Institute (Davis, n.d.), the Multiple Affect Adjective Checklist (Gotlib & Meyer, 1986), our clinical experience, and other words that our participants have used to describe their experiences.

6.2 PRACTICE: Values in our life story

This practice is a modified version of the technique "Your life in thirds," by Weiss (2018). For this practice, you will be looking back at your life story in three different segments. This means, for example, if you are 30 years old, then each of the segments of this line will symbolize 10 years of your life, and if you were 45 years old, each of the fragments of the line would symbolize 15 years of your life.

6.2.1 Looking at your life story in thirds

Estimated time: 9–12 minutes

Write a summary about the main events and memories that characterize each of these life segments, which correspond to roughly one-third of your life (see Table 6.2). Remember that you can decide for yourself what feels ok to write down or not. We also encourage you to balance the challenging or difficult memories, with some others that are positive or valuable for you. Try your best to find at least a couple of memories each of a positive or negative type, as nothing is too small to be worthy of attention. It can be the first time you tasted a food/drink you like, a landscape that awed you, the words from a friend/movie/song that gave you motivation– or bigger life events that shaped who you were, are, or are becoming, such as the memory of farewell of a person dear to you, relocating to a new city, or the transition between career paths.

Table 6.2 My life in thirds

My life from birth to...	My life from ... to ...	My life from.... to the present date

Guidelines for Group Practice

(L) Estimated time: 30 minutes

If you are using this workbook as part of a writing group, you will practice in a dyad or in a group of three (use break-out rooms if working online). Assign turns for who will start being the listener, and who will start sharing. If necessary, plan also who would have the next turn sharing. Assign someone the responsibility for setting an alarm to track time and ensure that each person in the group has an even time to share. The facilitator might give reminders about time, to help you stay on track.

While listening to one another, follow these guidelines:

- Each member will have 5 minutes to share with one or two others about their timelines.
- *For the person sharing*: Remember to take care of your personal boundaries and choose what feels ok to share and what you prefer to keep for yourself.
- *For the person listening*: While listening, please take notes about the possible *values* you feel could describe the speaker based on their storyline. These values might be implicit rather than explicitly written or spoken, so we are asking you to read between the lines of their sharing. Mind the urge to make this a conversation; this is an active listening practice that *does not call for questions or discussion about what is being shared*. You will have only 2 minutes to share what these values were, so we are asking you to be concrete by saying, for example:
  - *Thanks for sharing. Based on what you shared, I perceived you as a [Insert 3–4 values from Table 6.3, or values that are not in the table but that you feel describe the speaker.]*
  - *Would you like to share X part of your story with the whole group when we return? It is fine to say no.*

- Take turns sharing and listening, and make sure that each of you has the same time, as the facilitator will remind you.

Guidelines for one-to-one facilitation

In one-to-one facilitation such as peer-support or counseling, you can share with the facilitator what you feel comfortable summarizing from the "Life in thirds" exercise. Then, the facilitator will listen mindfully and share with you the values that they noticed while listening to your story.

Table 6.3 Suggested values that describe the person

Values				Other values not present in the list (please add)
Adventurous spirit	Dignity	Integrity	Patience	
Authenticity	Endurance	Justice	Self-respect	
Balance	Fearlessness	Kindness	Self-compassion	
Clarity	Flexibility	Modesty	Spontaneity	
Courage	Generosity	Loyalty	Reliability	
Compassion	Gratitude	Loving-kindness	Resilience	
Dependability	Hope	Perseverance	Trust	

Note: These values in the table are examples of those shared by the parents we have worked with, and values we have found useful in our clinical practice. As specified in the table, we encourage you to describe other values on your own as well.

6.2.3 What did you notice?

🕐 Estimated time: 3 minutes

What did you notice when writing during this practice?

Guidelines for Group Practice

🕐 Estimated time: 15 minutes.

If you are using this workbook as part of a writing group, you will have an opportunity to share with one another what they noticed while undergoing this practice reflecting about how the life we have lived can or not affect the way we grief, and how our grief can lead to resilience in the future.

Learning Theory Together

🕐 Estimated time: 10 minutes

Finding a meaning through anger, guilt, and shame

The death of a child is by definition tragic and typically perceived as assaulting our core sense of meaning as it contradicts the presumably normal cycle of life. Such loss can then give room for us into anguishing and seemingly endless questions, such as:

Why did this happen to my child? Did I do something wrong? or even, *Is this some sort of punishment that I deserve for my previous acts or shortcomings?* Most of the bereaved parents we have worked with have struggled with such questions, in a sense finding an answer to the corrosive "why" question by blaming themselves. But of course, this "answer" comes at a great price, registered in guilt, remorse, or shame.

Guilt and shame could be experienced in similar ways. However, while *guilt* tends to arise when we realize that we have made a mistake and that such a mistake has an impact on others, *shame* is more related to feeling that we are wrong as a person, that we are unworthy or less valuable than others (Greenberg & Iwakabe, 2011; The Emotion Compass, n.d.)

As an alternative to this ruminative, circular, and commonly destructive pursuit of an explanation for the loss at our own expense or that of others, we want to introduce two other questions, inspired by the work of the Austrian psychiatrist, neurologist, and philosopher Viktor Frankl (1969/2014), that might help you find a sense of meaning or direction despite the physical absence of your child in your daily life:

- What is this tragedy trying to teach me about life, about the human condition?
- How could this tragic experience become valuable for someone else? Or, in other words, how could I use my suffering in the service of others?

The answers to these two questions cannot be forced, as they are perhaps some of the most difficult questions human beings can encounter. Be gentle with yourself because the answers you find, if any, must be genuine and part of your process of attending to the wisdom beneath the feelings, the thoughts, the images, and the sensations that arise as you work with grief.

_____

_____

_____

_____

Writing through and beyond "VERB"

According to Baker and Stauth (2003), as we cope with suffering after a catastrophe, it is human to convey a first version of the happenings – here called "first story." Here we adapt their model, recognizing that in this initial account, we tend to describe what is happening to us according to the acronym, VERB:

VERB

- **V**ictimized: feeling helpless coping with fate or misfortune
- **E**ntitled: feeling we have the right to something different
  Rescued: a wish or fantasy of being rescued or spared, magically reversing the terrible event
- **B**laming: feeling a strong impulse to blame others or ourselves for our misery and unhappiness

There is nothing wrong with this first story unless we get stuck in it and do not move to the "second story" which moves toward finding meaning in suffering, accepting, and opening to the possibilities of making the best we can with the life as it is in each moment.

6.3 PRACTICE: A dialogue with shame

Estimated time: 10 minutes

For this practice, we ask you to write an imaginary exchange between two different aspects of your identity. One of these characters will be in contact with "the first story" as explained above. The first character is feeling victimized, entitled, wanting to be rescued, and/or blaming others or the self about the death of your child. The second character in this letter is connecting with the "second story," showing a sense of compassion, and pursuing possible answers to the question, *What is grief teaching me about life?*

NOTE: There are at least three ways to carry on this practice. One alternative is to can write this exchange using a first-person approach, such as stating, "A part of me is feeling that…, and there is another part of me that thinks/feels…." Yet, some people find it easier to write using a third-person approach, for instance "He/she/they felt at first that… and then, he/she/they started to consider that…." Alternatively, you can write this as a correspondence between the two voices, writing first from Shame, Anger, Guilt, the Victim, etc., and then responding with a letter to this character from another more oriented to the second story, which you might label the Searcher, Rationality, Wisdom, the Existentialist, etc. Sometimes speaking to yourself in a new and clearer voice is more helpful than a simple description of muddled emotions.

_____

_____

_____

_____

_____

_____

_____

_____

_____

_____

_____

_____

_____

_____

_____

_____

_____

_____

_____

_____

_____

_____

_____

_____

_____

_____

_____

_____

6.3.1   What did you notice?

🕐 Estimated time: 3 minutes

What did you notice when writing during this practice?

Guidelines for Group Practice

🕐 Estimated time: 15 minutes

If using this workbook as part of a writing group, you will have an opportunity to share with one another what you noticed while undergoing this practice.

6.4   Check out journaling

🕐 Estimated time: 4 minutes

Now that we are finishing this week's session, use some minutes to answer the following questions, without thinking too much about what you are to write. Answer in a way that feels spontaneous and genuine for you.

What have I learned about grief today?

_____

_____

_____

What have I learned about writing today?

_____

_____

_____

What have I learned about myself today?

_____

_____

_____

6.5   Further practice

Estimated time: 4 minutes

6.5.1   The first page of your autobiography

If you were to write an autobiographical novel, what would the first page of the novel look like? Write a draft of such a page. Try not to censor yourself, and not to overthink while you write. If you think it can be of help, use some of the tools you have learned so far, such as the proprioceptive question (page 17, chapter 1) "what do I mean by X? By X, I mean…"; or writing in third-person (Page 79, chapter 5).

_____

_____

_____

_____

_____

_____

_____

_____

_____

_____

_____

_____

_____

_____

_____

_____

_____

_____

_____

_____

_____

_____

_____

_____

_____

_____

_____

6.5.2   *Taking perspective*

Estimated time: 4 minutes

What emotions, if any, appear in the scene?

_____

_____

_____

What emotions are more silent and if these emotions had a voice, what would they say?

_____

_____

_____

What values would you like your readers to use when describing what you write? Rewrite the first page of the story aiming at making some of these values more explicitly visible in the text.

_____

_____

_____

Chapter 7

Meaning in life

Weekly theme(s): Psychoeducation and experiential learning practices about meaning in life, and narrative therapy.

Estimated length of a group session: 2–2.5 hours, including two pauses of about 10 minutes each.

Embracing compassion: We are about to embark on the last major module of this writing course, and this might be a bittersweet experience. We hope you can acknowledge all the good work you have done by now! Writing is an ongoing tool of self-exploration and support that you can take with yourself and keep applying it to grief and or other circumstances in your life.

Gentle reminder: We calculated the timeframes and the intensity that we indicate for each assignment based on our experiences facilitating online groups of therapeutic writing for bereaved parents like yourself. In case you are using this workbook on your own, without the support of a facilitator or a group, it is essential that you listen to your own emotional rhythm and write at your own pace. Take pauses when necessary and, ideally, use this workbook together with someone, be it a peer, a counselor, or a clinician. Check our suggestions on page 2-4.

DOI: 10.4324/9781003423270-8

7.1 Warm-up

7.1.1 Meditative writing

🕐 Estimated time: 5 minutes

Guidelines for Group Practice

If you are using this workbook as part of a writing group, in an online setting, you can turn off your camera while you write, if you feel it will help you to be more present in your reflections. The facilitator will let you know when is a minute left before returning to the whole group, and then you can turn your camera on again.

🔊 In case you want to listen to this meditation, follow this link to find a recording.

For the next few minutes, bring your awareness inward, step by step.

Notice first your surroundings and briefly write about them. Describe the physical place where you are right now, as you transition into writing practice. Are there any colors, shapes, or objects that call your attention? Do you notice any smell, sound, or texture?

_____

_____

_____

Now, when you are ready, bring your attention to your body as it sits wherever you are. What parts of your body are in contact with the chair? How do you know that your body is in contact with the chair? Are there any physical sensations you can notice, such as warmth, coolness, a tingling sensation, or even pain?

Write down what you notice.

_____

_____

_____

Is there something you need to do to feel more comfortable as you sit?

_____

_____

_____

Now, bring your attention inwards, and list the thoughts that pass through or spin around in your mind. Are there any worries, concerns, images, or memories that arise?

_____

_____

_____

_____

Notice if there are any emotions present for you right now. At times, it is easier to notice what we "don't feel" than to know what we feel! It is also okay if today you feel rather numb or quiet. Thus, write down any emotion that is dominant, absent, or name the numbness or quietness. For writing, all you need is to begin wherever you are.

_____

_____

_____

_____

Now, set one or two intentions for today's practice. Examples of such intentions are as follows:

General intentions when writing

- To be as present as possible during today's session.
- To feel closer to my child as I write.
- To tolerate uncomfortable emotions that can arise during the session.
- To take care of myself, and write at my own pace today, even if this means to take a pause from writing.
- To create something raw, honest, and or beautiful.
- Fill in this space with another intention if you find a personal one that is not mentioned above.

Specific intentions for the week's theme

- To be curious about the ways in which connecting with my child through writing can convey meaning to my life.
- To trust that even in the times where I find no meaning in my experiences, there is a meaning and a purpose in my life.

My intention for this week's practice is:

_____

_____

_____

_____

7.1.2 Check-in

🕐 Estimated time: 4 minutes

Sometimes we think that we do not have a right to feel certain ways about loss, or about our struggles to go about everyday life activities, this course included. This check-in is an opportunity for you to have an honest dialogue with yourself, as well as an opportunity to allow yourself to feel whatever you are feeling with compassion and acceptance. We will do this check-in each week, so you can have an overview of what you notice and learn about your emotional world throughout the course.

Give yourself a chance to fill in the first words that arise in your stream of consciousness. There are no right or wrong ways to feel, so do not think too much over the answer, and let words come to you with as little judgment as possible.

Throughout this program of therapeutic writing all feelings are welcome because being aware and turning toward those feelings with curiosity and compassion will guide you in finding the themes, scenes, and lines in your writings. We are expecting that, at times, it will be difficult to find a word that is accurate enough about the way you feel and therefore we have also made a table (Table 7.1) that can serve you as inspiration to fill in the blanks for this practice.

- I feel _____ and
  _____ about my grief today.
- I don't feel _____ and
  _____ about my grief today.
- Today I feel, _____ and
  _____ about the writing course.
- Today I DON'T feel, _____ and
  _____ about the writing course.

Table 7.1 Suggestions for emotions for the weekly check-in practice

Possible emotions				Other emotions not present in the list (please add)
Adaptable	Confused	Jealous	Peaceful	
Agitated	Critical	Joyful	Pensive	
Alienated	Content	Light	Pessimistic	
Afraid	Curious	Loving	Positive	
Angry	Distressed	Lonely	Relaxed	
Annoyed	Disturbed	Mad	Relieved	
Anxious	Empty	Melancholic	Resistant	
Apathetic	Euphoric	Miserable	Sad	
Ashamed	Excited	Mixed up	Safe	
Brave	Frustrated	Motivated	Serene	
Bitter	Gloomy	Mortified	Skeptical	
Bored	Grateful	Moody	Strong	
Bittersweet	Guilty/ Remorseful	Nauseated	Uncertain	
Calm	Happy	Negative	Unhappy	

(Continued)

Table 7.1 (Continued)

Possible emotions				Other emotions not present in the list (please add)
Caring	Hopeful	Nostalgic	Vibrant	
Cautious	Humiliated	Numb	Vulnerable	
Chaotic	Humbled	Optimistic	Worried	
Confident	Infuriated	Outside of myself	Weak	
Comfortable	Inspired	Overwhelmed	Wonderful	

Note: The list of emotions suggested in this table is inspired by the overview of emotional categories in English available at The Berkeley Well-being Institute (Davis, n.d.), the Multiple Affect Adjective Checklist (Gotlib & Meyer, 1986), our clinical experience, and other words that our participants have used to describe their experiences.

Learning Some Theory Together

Estimated time: 5 minutes

The Quest for meaning in life

As Viktor Frankl would say, being human is searching for meaning. We are wired for meaning, and yet often confronted with experiences that seem meaningless, such as the death of a child. While we are not destined to suffer endlessly, neither can we avoid experiences of suffering altogether. To be human is to be vulnerable to loss, and accepting death and dying as part of life is certainly one of the hardest challenges we face in our quest for meaning (Frankl, 2004). Both research and personal experience confirm that the tragic death of a loved one, and perhaps most particularly a child, can decimate our view that life "makes sense," that the future is reasonably predictable, and that we have some degree of control over the events with which we contend. When these "world assumptions" are shaken or shattered, we can be ushered into a long and anguishing course of grief as we strive to pick up the pieces and reassemble our worlds and our identities in the wake of such trauma (Neimeyer, 2019). Your efforts in this writing program can be viewed as an attempt to do just that.

Finding meaning through inevitable suffering is one of the most important quests we embark on as human beings. Many of us discover in this process that putting our suffering into service helps us turn a tragedy into a heroic journey (Frankl, 1975/1994).

According to Frankl (2004), we can find meaning and value through three main sources:

- By means of creating a work, a project, a relationship
- By means of experiencing or receiving something valuable, such as nourishment, beauty, support, acknowledgment
- Through our attitudes, especially toward circumstances that we have little control over, and that confront us with suffering.

We want you to pause for a moment and honor how remarkable it is that you are here, searching for meaning and motivation in a world that can be harsh and dangerous. It can seem paradoxical that we might need first to do things without feeling motivated before we can even find a clear sense of purpose beyond mere survival for the sake of ourselves or others.

7.2   PRACTICE: Revisiting the "Chapters of our lives"

During the first chapter of this writing course, you sketched the first draft of the table of contents of your memoir. Please **do not** go back just yet to check what you had written then! We would like you to give yourself an opportunity to write a new version of such a table of contents from the place you are at right now. Across the weeks, you've been working hard to explore your loss-related emotions, understandings, and implications for your sense of who you are in light of a profoundly significant life event. What description of your life feels most fitting now, perhaps even in the earlier chapters? After drafting a fresh version, you can compare both versions and see if any other insights come your way.

The instructions are the same as during the first week. We repeat them below:

7.2.1   *Finding titles for the table of contents in your autobiography*

Estimated time: 10 minutes

This is an adaptation of a technique developed by Professor Robert Neimeyer (2014).

Imagine you are 95 years old and are writing your memoir/autobiography. What would a table of contents look like? What would the headings for each of its chapters be? Write as many headings as you like, including chapters from all stages of life. You can create the titles for these chapters in the way that feels best for you! There are no right nor wrong ways to do this, as this is just the first draft for such a table of contents. While some people go for a chronological order of the chapters, others prefer to go back and forth in time such as some movies and or novels do. Some people also use chapter titles that are concrete and descriptive, while others choose titles that are more metaphoric and poetic. Do not overthink as you write, and start from the point in time that feels the most relevant for you.

Table of contents

1.

2.

3.

4.

5.

6.

7.

8.

9.

10.

11.

12.

13.

14.

7.2.2 *Time to take perspective*

🕐 Estimated time: 12 minutes

Now that you have written down your first draft of the chapters of your life, answer these follow-up questions. We encourage you to answer <u>at least 3</u> of the following questions, those that appeal to you the most. Note that these questions are a bit different than the ones you reflected upon the first time.

Organization

- When did the book of your life end, according to this table of contents? How might it look if you were to project ahead from the present, envisioning titles for future chapters to the point of your death or beyond?

Development

- If you were to group your chapters into broader sections phases of your life, each with a creative descriptive title, what might these be?

Theme

- In a big-picture sense, what would you say your life has been about? If someone asked you for a summary of the book in a single sentence, what would that sentence be?

Authorship

- If your child had been able to witness the whole of your life to this point, how would he or she describe your growth as a person? What sort of main character would your child cast you as, even as you embraced the tragedy of his or her death and whatever comes next?

Audience

- If you were to share the story of your life with other bereaved parents, what might they say about it, given their own partly parallel experience?

Framing

- If you were to give a title to your book, what would it be? If you were to choose art or an image for the cover of the book, what might this look like?

Write down your selection of the questions above and answer them.

7.2.3   Taking perspective

Estimated time: 5 minutes

Track back into your journal the pages where you sketched the first draft of the table of contents. Compare the two versions!

What do you notice as you compare them?

_____

_____

_____

_____

In which ways, if so, are they similar?

_____

_____

_____

_____

_____

How have your perspectives evolved, if so now that this writing course is coming to an end?

_____

_____

_____

_____

_____

7.2.4   What did you notice?

Estimated time: 3 minutes

What did you notice when writing during this practice?

_____

_____

_____

_____

_____

Guidelines for Group Practice

🕐 Estimated time: 15 minutes

If using this workbook as part of a writing group, each group member then will have an opportunity to share with one another what they noticed while undergoing this practice.

Learning Some Theory Together

🕐 Estimated time: 5 minutes

Continuing bonds

In the field of grief therapy, there is a theory called Continuing Bonds (Klass & Steffen, 2018). In a nutshell, this refers to the importance of developing a new and ongoing relationship with the person who has died, rather than focusing on "letting go" or "saying goodbye." Instead, from this perspective the goal is to retain rather than relinquish the relationship, not only changing it from a physical and concrete relationship to an inner and symbolic one but also one that can continue to have a place in the social world. In this case, it is about finding ways to continue your bond with your child rather than seek "closure." There are different ways to do so, such as practicing rituals of remembrance (e.g., visiting the graveyard, celebrating anniversaries of birth and death), displaying memorabilia at home (e.g., a portrait, a piece of clothing, a painting), speaking about them with others, or writing.

We encourage you to consider writing as a form of dialogue that can be continued over time. Nurturing your imagination and bringing dialogues forward with hope, compassion, self-compassion, loving-kindness, and a sense of meaning and purpose can help us overcome resistance and strengthen the relationship with your child, with yourself, with your partner, and with others.

7.3   PRACTICE: A letter to your child

7.3.1   *Bringing the acrostic back, as an inspiration*

🕐 Estimated time: 12 minutes

Use the acrostic that you wrote during the second week of this course as a starting point for writing a letter to your child/children. For example, you could start your letter by saying something like: *Some weeks ago, I wrote this to you.* But feel free to edit and update the acrostic if you want!

Then, proceed with the letter by completing at least 3 of the following sentences, which are part of the technique "Correspondence with the deceased" (Neimeyer, 2012a):

- What I now realize about grief is…
- I must admit that I still struggle with…
- I need to accept that…
- I want to remember you as…
- What I would want to tell you now is…

- In the coming weeks, I would like to…
- In the coming months, I'll need to…
- I want you to remember me as…

_____

_____

_____

_____

_____

_____

_____

_____

_____

_____

_____

_____

_____

_____

_____

_____

_____

_____

_____

_____

_____

_____

7.3.2   *Time to take perspective*

🕐 Estimated time: 10 minutes

How do you feel after writing this letter?

_____

_____

_____

_____

_____

Would you like to read it out loud to the group, or to the person who is accompanying you in this process?

_____

_____

_____

_____

_____

Is there any insight that you want to share about what happened?

_____

_____

_____

_____

_____

Gentle reminder: all feelings and emotions are welcome here. For many participants, this is a practice that is touching and vulnerable.

Guidelines for Group Practice

🕐 Estimated time: 15 minutes

If you are using this workbook as part of a writing group, each group member then will have an opportunity to share with one another what they noticed while undergoing this practice.

7.4   Check out journaling

🕐 Estimated time: 4 minutes

Now that you are finishing this chapter, use some minutes to answer the following questions, without thinking too much about what you are to write. Answer in a way that feels spontaneous and genuine for you.

What have I learned about grief today?

_____

_____

_____

What have I learned about writing today?

_____

_____

_____

What have I learned about myself today?

_____

_____

_____

7.5   Summarizing your own experiences

7.5.1   Overview of the check-in and check-out journaling

🕐 Estimated time: 10 minutes

In the following table (Table 7.2), summarize all that you wrote week by week during the check-in and check-out journaling practices. You might find these in your online responses or written in your journal week by week.

Table 7.2 Integrating perspectives from the check-in and check-out journaling practices

Week	Check-in: What I feel and what I don't feel	Check-out: Today I learnt....
1	I feel _____ & _____ about grief; & _____ & _____ about the course	_____ _____ about grief _____
	I don't feel _____ & _____ about grief; & _____ & _____ about the course	_____ about writing _____ _____ about myself

(Continued)

Table 7.2 (Continued)

Week	Check-in: What I feel and what I don't feel	Check-out: Today I learnt....
2	I feel _____ &_____ about grief; &_____ & _____ about the course I don't feel _____ &_____ about grief; &_____ &_____ about the course	_____ _____ about grief _____ _____ about writing _____ about myself
3	I feel _____ &_____ about grief; &_____ & _____ about the course I don't feel _____ &_____ about grief; &_____ &_____ about the course	_____ _____ about grief _____ _____ about writing _____ about myself
4	I feel _____ &_____ about grief; &_____ & _____ about the course I don't feel _____ & _____ about grief; &_____ &_____ about the course	_____ _____ about grief _____ _____ about writing _____ about myself
5	I feel _____ &_____ about grief; &_____ & _____ about the course I don't feel _____ &_____ about grief; &_____ &_____ about the course	_____ _____ about grief _____ _____ about writing _____ about myself
6	I feel _____ &_____ about grief; &_____ & _____ about the course I don't feel _____ &_____ about grief; &_____ &_____ about the course	_____ _____ about grief _____ _____ about writing _____ about myself

(Continued)

Table 7.2 (Continued)

Week	Check-in: What I feel and what I don't feel	Check-out: Today I learnt....
7	I feel _____ &_____ about	_____
	grief; &_____ & _____ about	_____ about grief
	the course	_____
	I don't feel _____ &_____ about	_____ about writing
	grief; &_____ &_____ about	_____
	the course	_____ about myself
8	I feel _____ &_____ about	_____
	grief; &_____ & _____ about	_____ about grief
	the course	_____
	I don't feel _____ &_____ about	_____ about writing
	grief; &_____ &_____ about	_____
	the course	_____ about myself

7.5.2 *Time to take perspective*

Estimated time: 4 minutes

When looking at this summary table, is there anything that has changed over time as you went about to follow this workbook? How would you describe these changes, if any?

_____

_____

_____

_____

What feelings and emotions are more dominant in this table? Which ones grew in frequency, and which diminished?

_____

_____

_____

_____

What do you feel might be important for you to continue working on, perhaps with the support of a peer, a family member, a counselor, or a therapist?

_____

_____

_____

_____

_____

Guidelines for Group Practice

Estimated time: 15 minutes

If you are using this workbook as part of a writing group, each group member then will have an opportunity to share with one another what they noticed while undergoing this practice.

7.6   PRACTICE: Closures and openings

Estimated time: 8 minutes

Now that we are at the final session of this writing program, we want to invite you to write a poem that starts with the following prompt. We would like you to write as spontaneously and genuinely as possible, without thinking too much about it.

A door opens …

Guidelines for Group Practice

Estimated time: 15 minutes

If you are using this workbook as part of a writing group, you will contribute with at least one line in the creation of a group poem. If you are working online, each participant can write their sentence in the chatbox, and the facilitator will collect the sentences and put them together, sharing in the chat a preliminary version of the poem. We have had positive experiences with this during the course.Then, everyone will be invited to suggest small edits, such as the order of the stanza, or words that can be changed to ease the rhythm of the poem, that everyone can comment on until a final draft is fully developed. If meeting onsite, then the facilitator can write the sentences down on a board.

Epilogue

Finding meaning in mourning

Throughout the preceding seven chapters of this book, we have provided you with relevant information about how grief feels, why it is difficult to integrate into our lives, and what to do about it. But beyond any instruction we have offered, we have encouraged you to investigate *your* grief — the experience of loss that is uniquely your own. We have also aimed at reminding you of your courage, strength, and resilience, as writing through grief might elicit difficult emotions, feelings, memories, and anticipations of the future, even as you reach for a future that includes but also goes beyond the tragic loss of your child. In this closing epilogue, we've tried to draw together some of the lessons from our research with other parents who participated in our groups, and whose responses helped shape the writing program you have just completed. We hope our summary of some of the "take aways" will be useful to you.

It is said that it takes a village to raise a child, and we also believe that it takes a village to mourn a child. We wrote this workbook to reassure you that you're not alone, no matter how difficult and painful grief feels. Therapeutic writing supports imagined dialogues with others and with parts of yourself and also can inspire conversations with those who read what you wrote. Over years of research in therapeutic writing, we keep confirming that writing is meaningful for those who engage in one or another practice because putting words to private experience not only helps people work through emotions, make sense of their suffering, and find meaning in life but also because of the sense of community and reciprocity crafted while writing together with peers (Lehmann et al., 2022, 2023; Lehmann & Brinkmann, 2019, 2023).

In Figure E.1, we illustrate the three dimensions of reciprocity that make writing such a powerful practice, as described in Lehmann and Brinkmann (2019). First, it facilitates self-exploration, helping us observe our inner world, get in touch with our suffering, with our strengths, and with different perspectives about our past, our present, and our future. Writing in a group also supports a sense of otherness, acknowledging that each person in the group might have their own path before, through, and beyond grief, and both reading and writing provide opportunities to share and listen to one another. This leads to the third dimension, a sense of togetherness as a group of peers, a deep sense of community and belonging that is anchored in specific values shared as the group dynamic develops. This is possible because of the vulnerability that each participant brings to the work, and for whom the writing group provides a safe haven and sounding board, with a sense of reciprocity and common humanity as a foundation.

Between 2020 and 2024, we had an ongoing dialogue with bereaved parents through the Norwegian SIDS and Stillbirth Society. They have provided us with written and oral feedback about the contents and structure of our writing courses, and some of them also gave us feedback about the Norwegian version of this workshop. We are also now training and

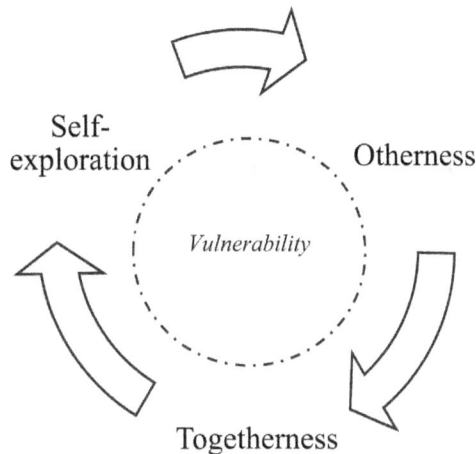

Figure E.1 Relational movements of reciprocity.

Reproduced with permission from Lehmann and Brinkmann (2019, p. 3).

supervising parents who want to use this workbook as part of peer support and counseling. In these final pages of this book, we want to share with you the key insights of our research, and our experience as grief theorists and grief therapists, as well as the possibilities for further development of therapeutic writing through grief.

There is more to grief than sadness. While sadness, longing, and nostalgia have been recognized as core dimensions of grief in psychology since the time of Freud (1917), grief is not a simple emotion, but rather a complex process in which diverse emotions comingle and coexist. Since the early stages of development of our therapeutic writing program, many of the users we worked with explicitly asked us about anger, guilt, shame, jealousy, and fear, just to name a few common emotions they encountered. These emotions were often powerfully present for them, but difficult to acknowledge, and they commonly felt that although friends, family members, and colleagues could sympathize with their sadness, speaking about these other more disenfranchised emotions remained taboo (Lehmann et al., 2022; 2023). Therefore, we explicitly constructed writing practices featuring anger, guilt, and shame in this book, and created check-in practices with a wide range of options to label emotions. In doing so, we wanted to convey a sense that although not all grief-related emotions are comfortable to feel or disclose to others, all can find a place and be given attention usefully in the privacy of expressive and reflective writing.

Knowing what grief is like can be soothing. Many of the bereaved parents we worked with appreciated learning what grief was like, such as how it could sneak into their daily lives in waves that were difficult to control. Learning about grief removed some of the fear, the guilt, and the shame: it became a reminder of a common sense of humanity as they shared the ambiguous feelings of grief, and the existential dimensions of loss that are not to be pathologized or avoided, but embraced and accepted with compassion (Lehmann et al., 2022).

Grief trajectories are unique, and nuanced by culture, gender, and our life stories. When we ran the first pilot versions of the writing groups we did not have any focus on gender in the advertisement of the courses. However, only women applied to the first courses. During a closing webinar about what we learned in one of these trial runs, a man raised his voice and shared that he very much wanted us to develop courses for men. We shared that wish, and therefore the next two courses we advertised were explicitly tailored for bereaved fathers. While the number of participants in these fathers' groups was small, the intensity of the sharing confirmed what some other scholars have previously indicated, that men and women tend to experience grief differently (e.g., Duka & Martin, 2010; Schut et al., 1997). For example, many of the men we worked with described a culturally reinforced sense of responsibility to take care or give room to their partners' grief. On the upside, this would be aligned with social expectations of men being the provider and having a supporter role. The downside was that this could also lead to avoidance of their own emotions, almost as if grief could be "frozen" for them (Lehmann et al., 2023). The groups became a safe space for many of these fathers to take their grief out of the freezer and thaw it in the warmth of exchanges with others.

Therapeutic writing is not for everyone, yet it works wonders for many. While we received very positive feedback from most of the course participants, we also received critical feedback that we used to improve this version of the workbook. When we began, we didn't have a workbook, per se, but rather a series of writing exercises that we ultimately refined and expanded. The workbook you have in your hands is the result of that back-and-forth exchange with bereaved parents, and we hope it is a resource that can support other writing groups, both for facilitators and bereaved parents. Our research findings highlight something that peer support organizations know in practice, bereaved parents have very different needs, and therefore the more different formats of support that are available, the better (Lehmann et al., 2022, 2023). Therefore, while this workbook might be useful for you or someone you know, it is also possible that you or others require additional tools to attend to grief in the depth it deserves, as you re-construct your life in the healthiest way possible. Unfortunately, and as we have also emphasized in our reports, far too many grievers do not have help available, and too often, the support that is available does not meet their needs and preferences (Aoun et al., 2015). We hope that this workbook expands this range, whether bereaved parents discover it as a resource for their private journaling, have it recommended to them by a counselor or therapist, encounter it in a professionally led writing group like those in our studies, or perhaps even adopt it as a structure for mutual support groups that they organize with others, online or onsite.

There is more to therapeutic writing than this workbook. We tailored the practices in this workbook as much as we could to the experiences of bereaved parents, although we are aware that there are many more techniques available that can be of use. Robert Neimeyer, co-author of this workbook, has developed and collected many more techniques such as the ones available in the following books (Neimeyer, 2012b; 2016; 2022; Thompson & Neimeyer, 2014). Even though these books are oriented principally to therapists and counselors, they are very readable, and provide many dozen additional methods that can help grieving people "live beyond loss" (Neimeyer, 2024), using poetry, fiction, journaling, storytelling, imaginal dialogues, correspondence with the loved one, and many other creative methods.

Whatever the format, the techniques of therapeutic writing have been extensively used in grief therapy and in cases of trauma or health promotion interventions (e.g. Den Elzen et al., 2023; Neimeyer, Smid & Comtesse, 2025; Pennebaker & Smyth, 2016), and we hope you find them equally valuable.

Choose the format that works for you. Our work to date has been mostly in groups, yet many families we are in contact with have expressed their interest in using writing as a form of self-help, or integrating it into their individual sessions of counselling or peer support. While we do not have enough data about this yet, we have created an anonymous link where you can share your experiences (https://no.surveymonkey.com/r/9GMRSY6)

If you decide to start a mutual support group online or onsite, we'd appreciate it if you could inform us through the site linked here. Perhaps we can even help with your recruitment, or provide training and supervision.

Consider the future of your writing. As an author of your very own "book of grief," which you have written across the course of this program, remember that you can continue to edit and expand these initial drafts because your writing will grow and change as you do. Re-reading what we have written can also provide perspective on where we were, where we are now, and where we are going. Some of the parents who attended our courses and then gave us feedback on this workbook said that at times they repeated some of the practices, gaining different perspectives each time. As for the question of what to do with your writings, this requires patience and consideration. While some participants find affirmation and useful, compassionate responses in sharing what they have written with their families or on social media, other participants prefer to keep their manuscripts as private as possible. Remember that once your text is published it is difficult to take it back, so make sure that you have spent enough time in writing, re-reading, and editing your text so that it feels both honest and solid enough to share selectively or publicly. The goal of practicing therapeutic writing is not to become an award-winning author, but instead to process emotions associated with challenging experiences, and find meaning in life in the process.

Draw on the power of peer-support. Our study participants consistently noted that being part of a writing group was one of the most valuable aspects of the experience, one that gave them a safe place to explore their own grief and journey toward a changed future, as well as a way to learn from the experiences and perspectives of others. So it is not only writing, but writing with others, listening, and sharing with one another, that counts. In this sense, your personal writing is a conversation starter. There are of course some challenges such as finding a schedule that works for you and other possible group members, and we scheduled our courses in the evening time, for maximum convenience. Our hope for you is that if you too want to find a community to support your writing practice, one will materialize, or perhaps be arranged (and shared with us!) by your own efforts. We provide a list of different organizations we are aware exist in different countries on the next page. Many of the parents we have worked with have found motivation in supporting others, finding meaning through service as Frankl (1986/2004) points out. However, neither writing nor group work is right for everyone, which leads us to our final point.

Be open to receiving additional support. Grief is not difficult because you are sick or crazy; grief is difficult because you have been through one of the most terrible tragedies a person can go through: losing a beloved child. It is human to grieve, and yet we can never be prepared enough for the suffering that it can entail. As therapists, we are often impressed by the resilience, courage, and strength of the people we work with. At the same time, as much as human beings are equipped to cope with tragedies and have the capacity to grow beyond traumatic and life-limiting experiences, it is important to be humble, recognizing that an extra level of support is sometimes necessary. While writing can help promote our mental health and well-being, it is rarely the whole answer to the questions posed by our losses. If across the months, you continue to feel stuck in preoccupying thoughts and feelings of grief, if you struggle to sleep, to get back to work or school, if you feel isolated or alone, please reach out to a professional therapist for the perspective and support you need. In this case, writing through bereavement can be the first step toward rebuilding life after loss, rather than a final destination.

A closing thought

Dear parent,

Thank you for being part of this writing journey. You have been brave and courageous. It is usual to struggle with significant feelings when we grieve. Remember that you are not alone. We also want to encourage you to look for support if you recognize that you feel stuck in one or another way after using this workbook.

Reach out to a hotline, your family doctor, or an online support community in your country, such as:

- Charlie's Kids, UK https://charlieskids.org/
- Cruse, UK [https://www.cruse.org.uk/]
- Held in Our Hearts, UK [https://heldinourhearts.org.uk/]
- The Lullaby Trust, UK https://www.lullabytrust.org.uk/
- Anam Cara, Ireland https://anamcara.ie/resources/helpful-links/
- Marie Curie, UK https://www.mariecurie.org.uk/
- SANDS Saving babies´ lives. Supporting bereaved families: https://www.sands.org.uk/
- MISS Foundation, USA [https://www.missfoundation.org/]
- Bereaved Parents of the USA [https://www.bereavedparentsusa.org/]
- First Candle, USA [https://firstcandle.org/]
- Red Nose, Australia https://rednose.org.au/
- Ciao Lapo, Italy https://www.ciaolapo.it/?lang=en
- Semi per la SIDS, Italy http://www.sidsitalia.it/
- Naitre et Vivre, France https://naitre-et-vivre.org/
- Swedish Infant Death Foundation: https://www.spadbarnsfonden.se
- Forældre og sorg - The Danish Association:https://foraeldreogsorg.dk/
- The Norwegian SIDS & Stillbirth Society: www.lub.no
- GISS center, global initiative https://gisscenter.org/
- The Compassionate Friends [https://www.compassionatefriends.org/] in many countries.
- Search for RENACER groups, led in many Spanish-speaking countries based on the work of Gustavo Berti and Alicia Schneider

Note: There might be many more organizations worldwide, we only name those we are aware of existing.

In addition, the internet abounds with support resources for many distinct forms of child loss, from cancer and rare diseases to suicide and homicide. You might make contact with more than one, and choose the one that feels right to you. Be aware, however, that counselors and therapists who specialize in parental grief can be a great help if these mutual support services are not enough. If you decide to reach out to them, we hope that the reflective writing you have done in this program gives you a clearer idea of what you need, and you might find continued journaling along these lines to be a useful adjunct to your therapy.

References

Al-Mahdy, D. (2001). *"The Guest House", by Jalal al-Din Rumi, translation. Retrieved from www. dinaalmahdy.co.*

Aoun, S. M., Breen, L. J., Howting, D. A., Rumbold, B., McNamara, B., & Hegney, D. (2015). Who needs bereavement support? A population based survey of bereavement risk and support need. *PloS One, 10*(3), e0121101. https://doi.org/10.1371/journal.pone.012110

Baker D., & Stauth C. (2003) *What happy people know*, New York: St. Martin's Griffin.

Burns, D. (1980). *Feeling good: The new mood therapy*. New York: Bantam.

Chozen Bays, J. (2017). *Mindful eating: A guide to rediscovering a healthy and joyful relationship with food. Revised edition*. Shambhala.

Corrigan, F. M., Fisher, J. J., & Nutt, D. J. (2011). Autonomic dysregulation and the Window of Tolerance model of the effects of complex emotional trauma. *Journal of psychopharmacology (Oxford, England), 25*(1), 17–25. https://doi.org/10.1177/0269881109354930

Davis, T. (n.d.). List of Emotions: 271 Emotion Words (+ PDF). Retrieved by: https://www. berkeleywellbeing.com/list-of-emotions.html

Den Elzen, K., Neimeyer, R. A. & Breen, L. J. (2023). Rewriting grief following bereavement and non-death loss: A pilot writing-for-wellbeing study. *British Journal of Guidance & Counselling*. https://doi.org/10.1080/03069885.2022.2160967

Doka, K. J., & Terry, L. M. (2010). *Grieving beyond gender: Understanding the ways men and women mourn*. Taylor and Francis.

Duffey, T. (Ed.). (2007). *Creative interventions in grief and loss therapy: When the music stops, a dream dies*. Taylor & Francis Group.

Edwards, J. (Ed.). (2017). *The oxford handbook of music therapy*. Oxford University Press, Incorporated.

Frankl, V. E. (1969/2014). *The will to meaning. Foundations and applications of logotherapy*. New York: Plume. Penguin Group.

Frankl, V. (1975/1994). *El Hombre doliente. Fundamentos antropológicos de la psicoterapia*. Barcelona: Herder.

Frankl, V. (1986/2004*). The doctor and the soul. From psychotherapy to logotherapy*. Souvenir Press.

Freud, S. (1917). *Mourning and melancholia*. The standard edition of the complete psychological works of Sigmund Freud, 14(1914–1916), 237–258.

Gotlib, I. H., & Meyer, J. P. (1986). Factor analysis of the Multiple Affect Adjective Check List: A separation of positive and negative affect. *Journal of Personality and Social Psychology, 50*(6), 1161.

Greenberg, L. (2006). Emotion-focused therapy: A synopsis. *Journal of contemporary psychotherapy, 36*, 87–93. https://doi.org/10.1007/s10879-006-9011-3

Greenberg, L. S., & Iwakabe, S. (2011). Emotion-focused therapy and shame. In Dearing, R. L., & Tangney, J. P. (Eds.), *Shame in the therapy hour* (pp. 69–90). American Psychological Asso5ciation. https://doi.org/10.1037/12326-003

Hedtke, L. (2012). *Bereavement support groups: Breathing life into stories of the dead* Chagrin Falls, OH: Taos Institute Publications.

Hermans, H. J. M. (2001). The dialogical self: Toward a theory of personal and cultural positioning. *Culture & Psychology, 7*(3), 243–281.

Hermans, H. J. M., Kempen, H. J., & Van Loon, R. J. (1992). The dialogical self: Beyond individualism and rationalism. *American Psychologist, 47*(1), 23–33.

Klass, D., & Steffen, E. M. (Eds.). (2018). *Continuing bonds in bereavement: New directions for research and practice*. New York. Routledge/Taylor & Francis Group.

Kristensen, P., Dyregrov, A., & Dyregrov, Kari. (2021). Sorg og komplisert sorg (1. utgave.). Fagbokforlaget.

Lehmann, O. V. (2018). Meaning focused perspectives on suffering, compassion, and caregiving for the elderly. A commentary on Schulz's & Monin's model. In Boll, T., Ferring, D., & Valsiner, J. (Eds.), *Cultures of care in aging* (251–269). Charlotte, NC: Information Age Publishing.

Lehmann, O. V., & Brinkman, S. (2019). "I'm the one who has written this": reciprocity in writing courses for older adults in Norway. *International Journal of Qualitative Studies on Health and Well-being, 14*:1. https://doi.org/10.1080/17482631.2019.1650586

Lehmann, O. V.; & Brinkmann, S. (2023). Virtuous ageing as a poetic endeavour: Motivations to write and effects of writing among older adults in Norway. In Lehmann, O. V., & Synnes, O. A. (Eds), *A Poetic Language of Ageing*. London: Bloomsbury Academi

Lehmann, O. V., R. A. Neimeyer, J. Thimm, A. Hjeltnes, R. Lengelle, & T. G. Kalstad (2022), Experiences of Norwegian mothers attending an online course of therapeutic writing following the unexpected death of a child. *Frontiers in Psychology, 12*, article 809848.

Lehmann, O. V., Kalstad, T.,G., & Neimeyer, R. A. (2023). Experiences of fathers in Norway attending an online Course on Therapeutic Writing After the Death of a Child. Qualitative Health Research. https://doi.org/10.1177/10497323231216099

Lengelle, R., & Meijers, F. (2009). Mystery to mastery: An exploration of what happens in the black box of writing and healing. Journal of Poetry Therapy, 22(2), 57–75. https://doi-org.ezproxy.uis.no/10.1080/08893670903072935

Lichtenthal, W. G., & Neimeyer, R. A. (2012). *Directed Journaling to Facilitate Meaning-Making, in R. A. Neimeyer, Techniques of Grief therapy: Creative practices for counseling the bereaved*. New York. Routledge.

Metcalf, L. T., & Simon, T. (2002). *Writing the mind alive: The proprioceptive method for finding your authentic voice*. Ballantine Books.

Neff, K. (2016). *Self-compassion. Stop beating yourself up and leave Insecurity behind*. London: Holder & Stoughton.

Neff, K., & Germer, C. (2018). *The mindful self-compassion workbook: A proven way to accept yourself, build inner strength, and thrive*. New York: Guilford.

Neimeyer, R. A. (1999). Narrative strategies in grief therapy. *Journal of Constructivist Psychology, 12*(1), 65–85. https://doi.org/10.1080/107205399266226

Neimeyer, R. A. (2006). *Lessons of loss: A guide to coping*. Center for the Study of Loss and Transition.

Neimeyer R. A. (2011). Reconstructing the self in the wake of loss: A dialogical contribution. In: Hermans, H. M., & Gieser, T. (Eds), *Handbook of dialogical self theory* (pp. 374–389). Cambridge: Cambridge University Press.

Neimeyer, R. A. (2012a). Correspondence with the deceased. In Neimeyer, R. A. (Ed.), *Techniques of grief therapy* (pp. 259–261). New York: Routledge.

Neimeyer, R. A. (Ed.) (2012b). *Techniques of grief therapy: Creative practices for counseling the bereaved*. New York: Routledge.

Neimeyer, R. A. (2014). Chapters of our lives. In Thompson, B. E., & Neimeyer, R. A. (Eds.), *Grief and the expressive arts: Practices for creating meaning* (pp. 80–84). New York: Routledge.

Neimeyer, R. A. (Ed.) (2016). *Techniques of grief therapy: Assessment and intervention*. New York: Routledge.

Neimeyer, R. A. (2019). Meaning reconstruction in bereavement: Development of a research program. *Death Studies, 43*, 79–91. https://doi.org/10.1080/07481187.2018.1456620

Neimeyer, R. A. (Ed.) (2022). *New techniques of grief therapy: Bereavement and beyond*. New York: Routledge.

Neimeyer, R. A., Smid, G. & Comtesse, H. (2025). Symbolic interactions, writing assignments and rituals. In Smid, G., Comtesse, H., & Boelen, P. (Eds.), *Psychotherapy for prolonged and traumatic grief: A guide for mental health professionals*. London: Routledge.

Neimeyer, R. A., Torres, C., & Smith, D. C. (2011). The virtual dream: rewriting stories of loss and grief. *Death studies, 35*(7), 646–672. https://doi.org/10.1080/07481187.2011.570596

Neimeyer, R. A., & Young-Eisendrath, P. (2014). Virtual dream stories. In Thompson B. E., & Neimeyer, R. A. (Eds.), *Grief and the expressive arts: Practices for creating meaning* (pp. 62–65). New York: Routledge.

Neimeyer, R. A., & Young-Eisendrath, P. (2015). Assessing a Buddhist treatment for bereavement and loss: The Mustard Seed Project. *Death Studies, 39*, 263–273. https://doi.org/10.1080/07481187.2014.937973

Palmer, P., & Scribner, M. (2017). *The courage to teach guide for reflection and renewal. 20th Anniversary edition*. Wiley.

Pascual Leone A., & Paivio S. (2013). Emotion-focused therapy for anger in complex trauma. In Fernandez, E. (Ed.), *Treatments for anger in specific populations: Theory, application, and outcome*. Oxford University Press.

Pennebaker J. W. (1993). Putting stress into words: health, linguistic, and therapeutic implications. *Behaviour Research and Therapy, 31*(6), 539–548. https://doi.org/10.1016/0005-7967(93)90105-4

Pennebaker, J. W., & Smyth, J. (2016). *Opening up by writing it down. How expressive writing improves health and eases emotional pain*. New York: Guilford.

Seip, Å. (2019). *Fra diktsamlingen: HER eller kunsten å huske hvem jeg er*. Heia Forlaget.

Shulz, R., & Monin, J. (2018). Suffering and compassion in older adult caregiving relationships. In Boll, T., Ferring, D., & Valsiner, J. (Eds.), *Cultures of care in aging* (pp. 213–242). Charlotte, NC: Information Age Publishing.

Schut, H. A., Stroebe, M. S., van den Bout, J., & de Keijser J. (1997). Intervention for the bereaved: Gender differences in the efficacy of two counseling programmes. *British Journal of Clinical Psychology, 36(1)*, 63–72. https://doi.org/10.1111/j.2044-8260.1997.tb01231.x

Stroebe M., Schut H. (2010). The dual process model of coping with bereavement: A decade on. Omega, 61(4), 273–289. https://doi.org/10.2190/OM.61.4.b

The Emotion Compass (n.d.). https://emotioncompass.org/

Thompson, B. E., & Neimeyer, R. A. (Eds.) (2014). *Grief and the expressive arts: Practices for creating meaning*. New York: Routledge.

Weiss, L. (2018). *How we work: Live your purpose, reclaim. Your snity, and embrace the daily grind*. New York: Harper Wave.

Index

Note: Page numbers in **bold** denote tables.

For Product Safety Concerns and Information please contact our EU
representative GPSR@taylorandfrancis.com
Taylor & Francis Verlag GmbH, Kaufingerstraße 24, 80331 München, Germany